What People are saying about

Seven Ages of the Goddess...

Seven Ages of the Goddess is a treasure-tr~   w writing
and thought about a very old su'   bject that
continues to inspire ext~   spiritual
expression. From the G.   1achina
of the current age, this bo   ..y expands
our notions of the Femal   ..r old world churns
through the recalibration c   .archal systems, this is a well-
timed addition to any thinking person's spiritual library.
H. Byron Ballard, author and senior priestess, Mother Grove
Goddess Temple.

Travelling from the Stone Age right through to the possible
future of goddess worship, *Seven Ages of the Goddess* brings
together some really interesting goddesses and their histories.
A veritable cornucopia of talented writers draw on personal
experience, historical text, folklore and even dip into fairy tales
to take the reader on a most wonderful journey. A fascinating
read.
Rachel Patterson, author of *Moon Magic*, *The Cailleach* and *Arc of
the Goddess*.

Wherever you are in your exploration and experience of the
goddess and what she means for you, *Seven Ages of The Goddess*
provides a beautiful and thought provoking journey through
Her ages offering a broad variety of perspectives and valuable
insights.
Antonella Hall, Founder Member - Norfolk Goddess Temple.
Priestess of Andraste, Priestess of The Goddess.

Love this fresh and new approach to Goddess in one book, between two covers! I have over 1,000 books in my library, thus very discerning about what I buy, but THIS BOOK will garner a place on my shelves!

Rev. Dr. Karen Tate, author, scholar, social justice activist and hostess of Voices of the Sacred Feminine radio.

This book is an essential introduction for those who are new to the idea of a female Godhead. We are currently living in a time of paradigm shift when the culture has begun to accept the idea of female equality and yet still seems mired in ambivalence about it. In the US only 20% of House and Senate members are women, despite the fact that women are just over half of the US population, and only 4.2% of Fortune 500 corporate CEOs are female. Women and men seem to be carrying an unconscious bias in favor of male leaders, which I suspect is ultimately due to the Biblical notion that divinity is male. Modern women carry a deep unconscious wound due to that philosophy, and men still assume privilege and superiority because of it. Even within these pages you can see the cultural ambivalence on display; "god" and "goddess" appear in some chapters while "God and "Goddess" appear in others. The Judeo-Christian-Islamic god is always "God", however. It is my hope that books like these will tip the balance so that the Divine Feminine can be appreciated, along with her male gendered partner.

Ellen Evert Hopman, author of *A Legacy of Druids - Conversations with Druid Leaders from the Britain, the USA and Canada, Tree Medicine Tree Magic,* the *Priestess of the Forest* Druidic trilogy, and other volumes.

Seven Ages
of the Goddess

Seven Ages
of the Goddess

Edited by Trevor Greenfield

Introduction by Jane Meredith

MOON
BOOKS

Winchester, UK
Washington, USA

First published by Moon Books, 2018
Moon Books is an imprint of John Hunt Publishing Ltd., No. 3 East Street, Alresford
Hampshire SO24 9EE, UK
office1@jhpbooks.net
www.johnhuntpublishing.com
www.moon-books.net

For distributor details and how to order please visit the 'Ordering' section on our website.

Text copyright: Trevor Greenfield 2017

ISBN: 978 1 78535 558 5
978 1 78535 559 2 (ebook)
Library of Congress Control Number: 2017945970

A CIP catalogue record for this book is available from the British Library.

Design: Stuart Davies

Printed and bound by CPI Group (UK) Ltd, Croydon, CR0 4YY, UK

We operate a distinctive and ethical publishing philosophy in
all areas of our business, from our global network of authors to
production and worldwide distribution.

Contents

Introduction

The Goddess.

Maybe you know her by one of her names, or by several of them. *Gaia, Ishtar, Inanna, Isis, Ceridwen, Mary, Selene, Kali, Green Tara, Freyja, Persephone, Oshun, Lilith, Durga...* and there are a thousand more names, or a thousand thousand. The Goddess goes far back, to a time before she had a name, before there were names.

At her broadest the Goddess is Earth itself, this beautiful planet we belong to. Each one of us has been formed from the atoms of the body of Earth, and each one of us returns back into this body at the end of our lives, as do the trees, the birds and animals, the insects, fishes, even the mountains and rivers. For some of us Earth – as grandmother, as mother, as sister, as lover – is a living being and we recognize her as Goddess in her life-giving properties. Earth, our home, is made up from the stuff of exploded stars. When we gaze up at night, above us, we see other stars, reminding us always that we are formed from stardust; that this coming into life and leaving it applies not just to creatures living on Earth but to Earth itself, and even to stars. Some of us know this whole process as the Star Goddess, and it is she who births all the worlds.

The Goddess may not be such a definite thing, in your experience. She might be an inner knowing, that you've always had, or that you are just now discovering. Maybe for you she is represented by someone in your life; your mother, grandmother, sister, lover or priestess. She might be expressed by a stage of life such as pregnancy and birth, or by an activity you undertake: gardening, painting, or healing. She may be a sense of presence that is just beyond where you have reached or what you have understood, something that is there in your dreams and then gone by the time you wake. She may be elusive, concrete, historical, mythical, occult or scientific.

Some of us lean towards the academic, we're drawn by discussions of history, archeology, comparative mythology or religion. Others of us come more alive in ritual, we engage in inner searching and rituals such as standing under the Moon's gaze and drawing her light down, into our bodies. Perhaps we are oriented towards dedication, promising to serve the Goddess, in a temple, a tradition or just in our own way. Maybe your heritage - magical or cultural or familial - draws you towards certain pantheons of deities, such as the Celtic, Hindu, Norse or Yoruba. We might be on the path of the initiate, the student, or the curious.

Who is the Goddess? What roles has she held, historically? How have other peoples understood her, and how do contemporary pagans, academics and goddess worshipers regard her? What meaning do those words, *the Goddess*, have for you?

Whether you start this book at the beginning and read through in the order presented, or you skip around, choosing pieces that catch your eye or draw your interest; whether you read it as a purely intellectual exercise, come at it from an emotional basis, or are curious, uncertain, already knowledgeable or experienced, this book will have something for you.

The Ancient Goddess, the mysteries of cultures long vanished and the remnants of temples, artifacts and myth remaining open this book. The Jewish Goddesses are the next of the seven Goddess ages presented here, and while for some of us that might seem a contradiction in terms, for others of us the names Lilith, Asherah and Sophia bring a smile to our faces. Mystery Goddesses – often those who have woven in and out of different times and places – are present, as writers offer reconstructions of the mystery religions which were often hidden even at the time, let alone to us now, looking back. In Christian Goddesses some delicate unpicking leads us to reconsider the two Marys of Christian myth, as well as female mystics of the Christian tradition.

Three further sections complete this book – Hidden Goddess, Re-awakened Goddess and Tomorrow's Goddess. In the Hidden Goddess we learn where and how the Goddess has stayed present in our culture, all along. Reading Re-awakened Goddess we might see the efforts and experience of ourselves and our contemporaries reflected back to us. Tomorrow's Goddess sets the imagination free, to roam, to question and to wonder.

The writings in this book can be an entry point, a confirmation, a provocation and a jumping off point for your own exploration, not just in reading these pages but in following threads laid down here, into the expansive world of Goddess writings; source material, theory, practical and fiction. Where will your reading take you?

Perhaps it will lead you to the doorway of an ancient temple - in a foreign country, in your own land or on the inner planes. Perhaps it will take you to a contemporary Goddess ritual - on the beach, under the full moon or in someone's living room. Perhaps it will intrigue you enough that you find workshops, conferences or groups, whether on-line or in person. Maybe you will send out a message to the Goddess, named or unnamed, asking her, or yourself, what place she has in your life. Perhaps your creativity will be touched by the works and ideas that are here, and your poetry, art, garden, child-rearing or music will feel the influence of the Goddess.

What will this book inspire in you? Turn the pages, read on, discover.

May the Goddess bless your journey.

Jane Meredith
July, 2017

Ancient
Goddess

Stone Age Goddess ~ Scott Irvine

She drifted aimlessly in the dark void; a dark mist of energy not knowing whether She was awake or asleep. She only knew that she existed. Then, very slowly at first She became aware of a pull on her energy from somewhere else that was attracted to Her and She knew that their coming together was imminent. She was filled with pleasure at the thought of merging with a new energy and felt a new force emerging in her consciousness; the force of LOVE. She and He combined causing them to expand creating Space and Time and the birth of the Universe. ~ An Ancient creation story.

I had been looking forward to this moment for a while; ever since I booked up a month in advance for a guided tour of the ancient underground goddess temple in the heart of Malta, the Hypogeum.

I was here because of a 12 centimetre long figurine made of terracotta discovered at this site 200 years ago. 'The Sleeping Lady' had sparked my interest and the fact that this tiny Mediterranean island and nearby Gozo had the largest concentration of goddess temples in Europe. I discovered there where over 40 goddess temples on the two islands constructed between 4,500 and 2,500 BCE. At the nearby Tarxien Temple, built 5,000 years ago the bottom half of a standing female figure carved in stone dominates the site. It is estimated to stand three metres tall if the top half was not missing.

The Hypogeum is cut into the top of a limestone hill using only stone mallets and antler picks and spread over three levels of interconnecting chambers linked by passages and stairways. The cool air inside was a relief from the hot Maltese sun. Controlled lights brought the chambers alive adding to the strangeness of the tunnels with their oracle holes, pits and spiral markings giving a sense of vulnerability mixed with a mild dread within the atmosphere of wonder and mystery.

When the goddess temples were in use Malta was an island at peace; a Stone Age Mediterranean paradise. According to archaeologist J. D. Evans life must have been easy otherwise they would scarcely have had the time or energy to spare to 'elaborate their strange cults and build and adorn their temples'. The temple builders and the population vanished abruptly around 2,500 BCE with no evidence of conquest or natural disaster. Where did the goddess and her followers go, and just as important, where did they come from? I needed to go back to the beginning of the Stone Age to where it all began.

The Stone Age is so named because it marked the moment when evidence of humans first manipulated the natural world for their own benefit using a thinking rational mind to create new things. Their skill, working in stone, to make everyday life easier improved throughout the Palaeolithic (Old Stone Age) era.

The Stone Age began around 400,000 years ago with the Lower Palaeolithic Period during which the ice age advanced and retreated continuously covering half the northern hemisphere for thousands of years at a time.

The people of the time, the Homo erectus (upright man), who had migrated out of Africa were family tribes working as a group to survive the cold conditions. These early humans had been around for the past 1.5 million years. They communicated in a guttural language and were the first hominoids to work flint utilizing its sharp edges alongside hand axes and bone hammers to make their lives easier. They lived in caves in the winter and temporary shelters in the summer when they followed the migrating herds of mammoth and elephants north, as did the lions, bears, wolves and hyenas. They took advantage of ripe fruits, nuts and plants they found as they traveled across the newly freed land from the ice. The earliest evidence of human created tools in Western Europe were discovered in Suffolk, England, when flint blades were found amongst human and animal bones dated to around 400,000 BCE.

The Middle Palaeolithic Period arrived around 200,000 years ago with Europe still in the grip of continuous waves of ice ages. A new race following Homo erectus out of Africa was the stockier larger brained Neanderthal whose existence lasted pretty much the length of the Middle Palaeolithic era. Arriving with them was the control of fire, enabling humanity to populate the colder northern realms of the world.

The majority of people today would consider the Stone Age as a harsh and savage environment but archaeological evidence suggests that early humans were sociable, capable and very tuned in to the rhythms of the universe. Both Homo erectus and Neanderthal would have had a very high perception of their world to survive the conditions, after all they had been roaming the land for hundreds of thousands of years and would have had a history handed down to them through the generations. Their consciousness was totally focused on the workings of not only the physical world but also the spiritual realm. John Mitchell in his book *The Earth Spirit: Its Ways, Shrines and Mysteries* describes the people of Old Stone Age as 'wandering under the direct guidance and protection of an earth spirit. Nature and all things in it drew their strength from the earth spirit. The spirit was life and was nourished by the stars, and in turn gave nourishment to everything in the land that required it'.

To the Stone Age people, the earth was seen as sacred and ruled by unseen spirits. Trees, hills, rivers, and springs were recognized as receptacles that contained the earth spirit. They saw the whole earth as a single living entity and would have been aware that it received fertility from the heat and light of the sun, becoming pregnant and giving birth to all life. Early humans saw that everything in the physical realm was a duality of opposing forces, a dynamic they understood to be at the essence of all creative processes.

There is evidence of ritual practices by Neanderthal in burying their dead in graves with stone tools and shells indicating their understanding of an afterlife or otherworld for the newly released spirit to journey to.

The Upper Palaeolithic Period is defined by the arrival of modern humans into Europe arriving from the Near East around 40,000 years ago. Originally from Africa but rather than follow the western coastal route into Spain like the races before, Homo sapiens (wise man) traveled east around the Mediterranean through Egypt, Palestine and Turkey into Greece. They brought with them a Stone Age Renaissance of art, ritual and magic, and with expanding language skills had improved social organisation and an understanding of symbolic thought. They saw the land as a blank canvas for new ideas and creativity. At the same time, Neanderthal went into decline and Homo erectus disappeared altogether.

The climate was getting warmer and the ice sheets less severe opening a fresh new world for the wanderers to discover, exploring and hunting further north than they had ever done before. Homo sapiens were aware of a higher force, greater than themselves existing in an invisible spirit world. To them everything cooperated towards balancing the whole such as dark and light, winter and summer, female and male. They saw the world of spirit as real and as important as the material world in which they existed. Natural born seers were chosen and highly trained as medicine men and women: shamans that could communicate with the spirits in order to guide the tribe, heal the sick and interpret dreams. Shamans were the intermediaries between the visible world and the hidden realm of the spirits.

The tribal communities were aware of the yearly cycle of the seasons and practiced a symbolic interaction between the tribe and the land where the tribe represented the masculine energy of the sky, and the land represented the feminine energy of the earth. Seasonal rituals were performed in honor of Mother Earth and Father Sun for the bounty they supplied and the continued fertility of both the tribe and the land. Humans began to carve objects in stone, reindeer antler, mammoth tusk and animal bone for the first time. A 40,000 year old sculpture of a lion was discovered carved from a mammoth tusk in Germany in 1931. Most of the earliest human-made figures are representations of the pregnant earth goddess. The 'Venus' of Willendorf, tinted in red ochre, the symbolic blood of rebirth, found in Austria was dated to around 24,000 BCE and the Kostenki 'Venus' from Russia was found to be carved about 23,000 BCE. According to Rachel Pollack in *The Body of the Goddess* 'man-made objects served as votive offerings, devotional objects for the Great Goddess'.

Human and animal birth was one of the great mysteries of the Old Stone Age. According to Peter Lancaster Brown in *Megaliths, Myths and Men*:

> The 'Venus' figures could have reflected the biological miracle of birth and be a symbolic meaning of birth and rebirth. They reflected the cyclic nature of the universe; the creation, the sustaining and the death of all things. It would not have gone unnoticed that the lunar cycle and the menstrual cycle had a similar time span.

These and thousands of other goddess figures have been found across Europe and the Near East which shows mankind were aware of the workings of the goddess in nature and symbolically brought her into the material world to dwell within the sculpture and cave art giving a physical form to the spirit presence. Goddess figurines were carved and their symbols painted on cave walls to venerate and instil goddess energy in the physical world. In *The Language of the Goddess* by Marija Gimbutas, 'early cave painters signified the goddess symbolically portraying breasts, vulvas, pubic triangles, cup marks and spirals on the walls.' The earliest cave art dates from 30,000 years ago reaching a pinnacle with the cave paintings at Lascaux in France and Altamira in Spain created around 17,000 years ago.

With a warming climate and retreating ice sheets opening up great tracts of fruitful land the Mesolithic period (Middle Stone Age) arrived with great promise and optimism around 12,000 BCE. Great forests of lime, oak, elm, birch, pine and hornbeam rich with wildlife and provisions dominated the landscape of Europe. Stone Age people were now making smaller flint tools: microliths used for sewing hide and boring holes in shells for jewellery.

At this time there existed a social order in which men and women had equal status, lived in harmony with nature with life centering on the worship of the Great Mother Goddess. The Earth was revered as the embodiment of the goddess and death was seen as a return to her womb. Egg shaped graves discovered in Slovakia around 7,000 BCE were believed to represent the dead reborn to the Earth Goddess. The Mesolithic people saw no division between the past and future or between life and death because the Goddess was all these things; this was indeed the Golden Age.

The land between Britain and the rest of Europe was a rich fertile oasis called Doggerland and home to hundreds of tribes living peacefully together according to science writer Laura Spinney:

These tribes would come together for an annual social event to hunt and feast. Young men and women from different tribes would find mates and the elders would exchange information. It would have been a simple life if childhood was survived. These people knew where they were in the landscape and in the universe and the role of the goddess in all of it.

Tens of thousands of figurines and other representations of the goddess, along with highly ornate pottery have been unearthed at sites all across Europe from the Mesolithic period. At Catal Huyuk, also known as Çatalhöyük, in Turkey, dated around 6,000 BCE shrines were dedicated to the Goddess. The site showed that rituals were conducted by priestesses while priests played only a minor role within the community. At the same time the construction of over 40 goddess temples began on the small island of Malta.

It was around this time, after millennia of slowly rising waters due to the massive release of melting ice, sea levels began to rise causing the tribes of Doggerland to migrate to higher land. A landslip on the sea floor off the coast of Norway triggered a tsunami that flooded the lowlands leaving Britain an island in the process.

Between 4,300 and 2,800 BCE the stability of the Golden Age came under threat from Middle Eastern tribes settling across Europe and gradually eroding the ancient cultural values of Old Europe. Early farming communities spread across the land and before long the goddess became a symbol of agricultural enterprise as the hunter gatherers began to settle in one place.

The Neolithic Period (New Stone Age) arrived around 4,000 BCE with a purpose never before seen introducing the Goddess worshippers into a new way of thinking. Making pottery and learning new farming skills, the Neolithic people found they no longer needed to roam the land in search of food. Tribes found a suitable place to settle down and stay forming larger societies and the need for hierarchies and control. The new settlers brought with them powerful priestesses who served as communicators between the spirit and material worlds releasing the community to clear the land of trees, quarry large blocks of stone and build stone monuments to honor the Goddess.

Long Barrow in Gloucester, UK, was built around 3,000 BCE which had stone walls leading to an entrance that resembled the open legs of the Goddess with the entrance made to look like a vulva. Other long barrows across Britain were representations of the lower half of the Goddess with a central chamber representing the uterus and the antechamber the vagina.

Also in the UK, discovered in a flint mine at Grime's Graves, East Anglia was an altar of flints with carefully placed pick axes made from deer antlers heaped around it. Set in front were chalk carvings of a pregnant woman, a phallus and chalk balls. Were these placed here to appease the Earth Goddess? To the New Stone Age mind every part of the earth was inhabited and directly ruled by the spirits. To harm the land in any way was like cutting into the Great Mother herself who as a result needed to be placated in some way. This was done by conducting a ritual to gain the blessings of the earth spirits and leaving an offering in the hope of avoiding her wrath. An enormous amount of building work took place in the landscape at this time including Silbury Hill, Wiltshire with Avebury stone circle rising shortly after.

Towards the end of the Neolithic Period another group of settlers arrived in Britain from the East around 2,000 BCE. We call them the Beaker People because of the style of their pottery. They were traders in goods and knowledge and brought with them their Sun and Nature God, Bel. Priest Kings replaced the priestesses in maintaining the spiritual well-being of the community, seducing them with ceremony and magic. Mankind began to believe that the material world was the only reality and the spiritual realm a mere reflection of the material.

The power of the Great Mother began to decline when men became aware of their role in creating babies thanks to their observation and skills in animal husbandry which led man to take control of his own destiny.

Stone Age thought was replaced by the nature of the male dominated conquest-seeking Bronze Age that arrived around 1,500 BCE. The Great Mother became the Babylonian Goddess Tiamat, a self-existing boundless watery mass. It was She who gave birth to space and time, heaven and earth and all life. Her world was an external cycle of creation, duration and destruction;

a living entity with a primary purpose to manifest potential in humanity. She possessed the Tablets of Destiny which gave her the power of control over the order of the Universe. After a fierce battle with the Babylonian Chief God, Marduk killed the Goddess cutting her body into pieces and scattered them across the world while taking the Tablets of Destiny for himself.

When God took control of the well-being of the masses, compassion became pity, love became dependence and spirituality became religion and dominance. Male assertiveness, direct action and intellect replaced female nurturing, sensitivity and intuition, Moon time was replaced by Sun time and the cyclic nature of the Goddess became the linear reality of the God. In time, Neolithic people came to live in obedience to God's command and laws.

The Mother Goddess was divided into separate and individual parts with each part having different personalities and power in an attempt to keep her hidden or at the very least subdued and inferior to the new Gods. But like the cyclic nature of the Stone Age Goddess, what goes around, comes around.

Cybele ~ Mat Auryn

Peering through the sands of time we find the Great Mother Goddess' roots stemming all the way to the prehistory of mankind's oldest settlements. The goddess Cybele is perhaps the oldest deity in Earth's history. Reaching all the way back from neo-Paleolithic prehistory to her height of worship in the classical period, we see her reverence even today among many modern day pagans and occultists. Despite strong attempts to wipe out her existence and her devotees by various patriarchal regimes, she persists.

Tracing the history and the myths of Cybele is no easy task. There are so many conflicting myths, accounts and records of her and her cults throughout time. This isn't made any easier with intentional destruction and attempts to erase her. Some say she was a witch of the mountains who became deified, while others say that she was the child of the sky and earth itself. The Greeks called her Meter Theon meaning Mother of the Gods while the Romans called her Magna Mater meaning Great Mother. It is undeniable though, that wherever she went she held a status of extreme importance, even amongst the other gods themselves.

Cybele's roots appear to originate as far back as 9000 BCE from the mountains of the ancient Indo-European people called the Phrygians of Anatolia, a region known today as Turkey. It is here in the hilltop sanctuary carved out of stone called Göbekli Tepe that we find reliefs of a mother goddess with a lion on each side rearing up towards her. It is later in the same region that we find similar iconography to a goddess with the inscription of her name Matar, meaning "Mother" and the epithet Kubileya meaning "Mountain".

Although no myths exist from this time period, primitive clay idols of a pregnant looking female deity seated upon a throne with large felines on each side was discovered in Çatalhöyük an ancient Neolithic settlement in southern Anatolia around 7500 BCE to 5700 BCE. The imagery is undeniably reminiscent of the Mother Goddess, which evolved in the Anatolian region, having the most important iconography of Cybele.

At the ancient Phrygian city of Pessinus near the base of Mount Agdistis, the Great Mother was greatly revered in the form of a black meteorite that fell from the sky. This object was viewed as such an important representation of the Great Mother that the name of the city, Pessinus, means "falling down" in reference to the meteorite. It is interesting to note that the famous goddess figurines of Çatalhöyük are remarkably similar to the Venus of Willendorf in Austria, at which were found talismans, amulets and ritual knives crafted from moldavite and other tektites beside the Venus. Tektites are natural glass formed from meteorite impacts. The black meteorite in Pessinus would later play an important role in the introduction of Cybele's cult in Rome due to Sibylline prophecy.

The Phrygian city of Gordion became an important center of worship of the Great Mother who came to be known as Cybele. Cybele was so important to the people of Gordion that she is the only deity that has been found to have any iconography in the city. It's interesting to note that the Hellenized worship of Cybele eventually began influencing Gordion's worship of her as well, the area that Cybele originated. The cult started to take on the Hellenized imagery of Cybele as time progressed. No longer was she a pregnant goddess with full breasts but now depicted as a more matronly goddess having an endomorph body frame and wearing a mural crown of city walls and towers from which locks of hair spilled out, just as her Hellenic counterpart.

Cybele's worship spread from Anatolia to the Aegean Coast and islands, and outward to Crete until it eventually made its way to Greece. It is around 600 BCE to 500 BCE that her main cult moved from Phrygia to Greece. By 400 BCE her worship was accepted and incorporated into Greek religion. She was welcomed into Athens as well as Alexandria, where she was worshipped by the Greek population as "The Mother of the Gods, the Accessible One" and "The Mother of the Gods, the Savior who Hears Prayers".

The temples of Ephesus became dedicated to her worship and the citywide ecstatic celebration called the Ephesia was performed in her honor. Some scholars even believe that the great Lady of Ephesus was really Cybele herself, having more attributes of the Anatolian goddess than the Roman goddess Diana and her Greek counterpart Artemis with whom Cybele was sometimes conflated and to which the statue is often named.

We see on the statues of the Lady of Ephesus a turret crown often reserved as iconography for Cybele herself, symbolic of her patron deity status within the Roman Empire. The statue has carved animals sacred to Cybele; on each side are representations of canines or felines, though much of them are destroyed so it's hard to be certain. It's interesting to note that the Lady of Ephesus has many breasts, symbolic of motherhood, which is odd for a virgin deity like Diana. Some historians theorize that they aren't breasts at all, but rather testicles, if so, it would make sense that Cybele would wear this as a symbol of her devotees' sacrifice and devotion to her through castration. It's also interesting to note that the word "Artemis" is only ever associated with her through Christian writings, but there are inscriptions to Diana. Remember that Diana translates as a feminine version of Dius – meaning God. Perhaps Diana was simply a title for the Lady of Ephesus stating that she was the Goddess.

It is also interesting that the historic hatred for Cybele by early Christians was only parallel to the hatred given to Diana of Ephesus. There is a graffiti inscription by early Christians at the Temple of Ephesus that states, "Destroying the delusive image of the demon Artemis, Demeas has erected this symbol of Truth, the God that drives away idols, and the Cross of priests, deathless and victorious sign of Christ." Even in the Bible, Acts, 19:24-35

17

slanders the Lady of Ephesus stating "What man is there that knoweth not how that the city of the Ephesians is a worshipper of the great goddess Diana, and of the [image] which fell down from Jupiter?" Which is fascinating because we know that Cybele was associated with a meteor that fell to Earth and Cybele was considered the daughter in many myths of an Anatolian sky god often referred to as Jupiter in Greek writings. The Bible also states "the great goddess Artemis will be discredited; and the goddess herself, who is worshiped throughout the province of Asia and the world, will be robbed of her divine majesty". This is also interesting since Cybele's worship was primarily originating from Anatolia, the part of Turkey, which was in Western Asia.

It is not just Artemis and Diana that Cybele was synchronized with in the ancient world. In the classical world Cybele was often conflated with several other goddesses including Rhea, Demeter, Aphrodite, Juno, Bona Dea, Helena and Hekate. The Thracians saw Cybele as the chief divinity of the islands of Lemnos, and Samothrace as Rhea-Hekate. The Samothracians themselves identified Iason and Demeter with Attis and Cybele. The Phrygians associated Rhea with Cybele where she was seen as the mentor and purifier of Dionysus curing him of the madness Hera cursed him with according to Apollodorus, which led to ecstatic Dionysian elements becoming incorporated with the worship of Rhea. Rhea's daughter Demeter was attributed to many qualities of Rhea and often the two beings seemed to have interwoven with each other. The worship and attributes of Cybele, Rhea and Demeter became so blurry and so confusing that ancient classical writers often interchanged these names.

However, her cult was not always accepted in the ancient world. We know that the Scythians did not accept her and there's record from Herodotus that the Scythian citizen Anacharsis traveled to Greece where he fell in love with Cybele and was put to death when he returned to Scythia for trying to introduce her cult there. The Romans who had adopted the Greek gods and conflated them with their own did not originally embrace Cybele or her cult with open arms. The worship of Dionysus and Cybele were seen as too wild to Roman authorities and the practice of castration, which was performed by Cybele's eunuch priesthood, was not only taboo but also an act that would revoke Roman citizenship of anyone who performed it. The Roman Senate initially banned the worship of Cybele seeing her as a threat to not only their social order but to their strongly held patriarchy itself.

It wasn't until 203 BCE that the Roman State began embracing Cybele and her cult although watering it down greatly. At that time Rome was engaged in its second war with Carthage. Crops were failing as famine spread across the land and there were many ominous omens such as meteor showers. The oracular verses from the Sibylline Books were consulted and stated that if a foreign enemy tried invading Italy they could be conquered and driven out only if Magna Mater was brought from Pessinus in Turkey to Rome. The Oracle of Delphi in Greece was consulted who conveyed the same information.

Cybele's sacred black stone meteorite was brought to Rome and a great Temple was built to house this stone on Vatican Hill for the purposes of worshiping Cybele. Emperor Trajan did so and they won the war. Under Emperor Augustus Caesar, Cybele became a wildly popular goddess among the Roman people, though Roman citizens were still prohibited from participating in her priesthood. Her Galli priesthood at the time consisted of slaves and foreigners, neither being Roman citizens. Emperor Claudius during the 1st century BCE lifted the ban and permitted citizens to be castrated up until the reign of Domitian during the 1st century CE who once again banned the practice.

The 2nd-century BCE Greek historian Pausanias states that Cybele was the child of a Phrygian sky father (whom he identifies with Zeus) and earth mother. The child was born third sex as a daimon named Agdistis who possessed both male and female genitals. Fearing the power of Agdistis the gods castrated the child whereby she became Cybele. The male genitals of Agdistis became an almond tree with ripe fruit. A daughter of the river Sangarius took the fruit and placed it in her bosom whereby she became pregnant with Attis. Young Attis was said to have been so supernaturally beautiful that the goddess Cybele took notice and fell in love with him. When he became an adult he was sent off by his parents to marry the King of Pessinus' daughter. During the commencement of the wedding ceremony, as the wedding song was being sung Agdistis-Cybele appeared and drove Attis and the King mad, causing them both to castrate themselves on the spot. Agdistis-Cybele felt remorse and persuaded Zeus to grant Attis immortality and agelessness.

Ovid writes that according to a Muse, Attis was so beautiful that Cybele made him her shrine's guardian. She demanded that he remain a virgin so as not to cheat on her; Cybele consequently granted him immortality. He promised to do so, swearing death if he broke the vow. Unfortunately he did break the vow with the nymph Sagaritis. Cybele, in fury, killed the nymph by slashing down her tree and drove Attis to madness where he took a jagged stone and cut off the part of his body that had betrayed his oath. This was the reason why the priests of Cybele castrated themselves, in likeness of her most beloved. The eunuch-priesthood of Cybele was known as the Galli and was renowned for their ecstatic rites which are said to have involved orgies, wine, intoxication, sacred prostitution, frenzied dancing and wild music, which is why Cybele is often depicted with a hand drum.

Hermesianax, the 4th- century BCE poet, according to Pausanias, wrote that Attis was born as a eunuch to Galaus the Phrygian. Attis moved to Lydia where he worshiped the Great Mother Cybele and celebrated in her orgies and quickly rose to great honor among them. So much so that Zeus grew angry at their celebration of Attis and sent a great boar to destroy the land of the Lydians. A group of Lydians, including Attis, was killed in the attack by the boar.

The 1st-century BCE Greek historian Diodorus Siculus wrote in the *Library of History*, Book III, the origins of Cybele as follows: Cybele was the offspring of King Maeon and Dindyme of Phrygia. Not desiring to have or raise a child, Cybele was abandoned upon Mount Cybelus. Through the protection of the gods, leopards, lions and other ferocious beasts discovered the infant. They wet-nursed her instead of devouring her. A shepherdess in the area saw the infant sucking on the teats of these animals and adopted the child, naming her after the mountain where she was found.

She was said to be beautiful and virtuous, inventing musical instruments such as the cymbals, kettledrums and reed pipes. She became a great witch and healer, teaching the people how to cure their children and their livestock, rites of purification and performing spells to save infants from death. She began to be greatly admired for this and people began to regard her as the "mother of the mountain".

When the lands of Phrygia had become infertile and wouldn't produce fruit any longer the people petitioned the gods. The gods instructed that Cybele was to be treated and honored as a goddess whereupon the people began erecting altars and performing rites to her and later built a temple to her during the rule of King Midas. Statues of lions and panthers were placed near statues of Cybele to honor their nursing of the infant who would come to be deified.

By the 4th century CE Emperor Valentinian II, the first Roman Christian emperor, banned the worship of Cybele, and those caught still worshipping her underwent extremely cruel persecution. Under Christian Emperor Justinian I in the 6th century CE, many of Cybele's temples were destroyed. Not only were people tortured for the worship of Cybele and participation in her cults but all their property and land was seized and they were often buried alive afterwards. Cybele's Temple on Vatican

Hill is now the site of the Vatican's Basilica of St. Peter. It's hard to imagine that this was accidental, but rather an act of Christian Patriarchy conquering Roman goddess worship, particularly a goddess as widely loved in Rome as Cybele. By the 6th century CE the cult of Cybele was completely wiped out under Christianity as demonic.

It wouldn't be a far stretch to consider that the Whore of Babylon from the Book of Revelations was a veiled depiction of Cybele, the Great Mother of Rome. Early Christian writers have written about this association as well. This speculation makes a lot of sense when you think about the origins of the Book of Revelations written by Christians in a Pagan Rome where Cybele was so greatly adored. The Whore of Babylon shares a lot of similarities with Cybele and her Galli. The Whore of Babylon is described as the Mother of (Sacred) Prostitutes, earth's inhabitants are drunk on her wine, she is referred to as the spirit of wildness and is depicted with a beast. Interestingly in the Sibylline Oracles the words "Rome" and "Babylon" are often used interchangeably.

It is also believed by some that the myth of Cybele giving birth to Attis as a virgin and the story of his death and resurrection was also seen as a competing threat to Christianity, as the myth was similar in a lot of ways to that of Mary and Christ. These parallels are noted by many late pagan writers as well as fathers of the early church. If this is indeed true and the Whore of Babylon was based upon the Roman Cybele, then we see her worship continuing in the form of Babalon in the religion of Thelema, the Scarlet Woman that Aleister Crowley wrote about in *The Book of the Law* based upon the Whore of Babylon of Revelations.

The Celts and the Divine Feminine
~ Jhenah Telyndru

The religion of the ancient Celts is a difficult topic to explore, for it requires that we piece together incredibly incomplete information from various source streams. As the Celts embraced a prohibition against committing their sacred beliefs and practices to writing, they have therefore deprived themselves of a direct voice with which to speak to history. Instead, we must look to the archaeological record, examine the biased reports of the Classical contemporaries of the Celts, and attempt to mine remnants of ancient belief systems from the Celts' surviving myths and legends which were redacted in the medieval period separated by time, religion and culture from the myth's progenitors. What remains is but a patchwork quilt tantalizing in its detail yet frustrating in its lack of wholeness.

While we cannot paint a clear picture of the religious beliefs of the ancient Celts, or know the details of the teachings of the Druids, we can cobble together what information we do have to speak in broad generalities. To do so, we must recognize the limitations of our sources – realizing that the archaeological record cannot address intention when it comes to prehistoric peoples, nor can we trust the contemporary writings of the Greeks and Romans about the Celts to be fully accurate and without bias or embellishment. Neither can we with certainty apply what is known from one Celtic region to the next, understanding that while there is a loose confederation of what constitutes Celtic culture, it is a mistake to paint these disparate people who existed through a wide distribution both of time and space as monolithic entities with the same beliefs and practices; indeed, even their languages had evolved separately into distinct branches and dialects.

The reason for this is that Celtic culture spanned much of

Western Europe, and included modern France, Spain, Ireland, Wales, and Britain. Their collective roots can traced back to the La Tene and Hallstatt cultures of Northern Europe, therefore, they shared a common sense of origin, a similar basis for language, related systems of belief, and an overall cultural identity. In addition to these spatial and linguistic separations, Pagan Celtic culture existed over a span of about a thousand years, from its origins in central Europe during the 8th century BCE, through to the final Christianization of Irish, Gaulic, and Welsh peoples during the 4th century CE. Because the myths and legends of the Celts remained in oral tradition until the 7th century CE in Ireland, and even later than that in Britain and France, it is difficult to know how much of the indigenous mythologies are present in these tales, and what parts are influenced by outside forces, such as Roman syncretism, and diffusion of elements of international popular tales from other European sources.

Although we cannot be sure, it is possible that as the Celts — or their culture, or both — moved out across Europe from their Le Tene homeland, they brought their Gods and their stories with them. These tales would have evolved over time, and regional variations would have developed based on the cultural needs of the different landscapes the Celts settled into, as well as some degree of influence from the beliefs and practices of the indigenous peoples of these lands. It is possible, too, that if Celtic culture spread not because of the physical movement of people, but due to the transmission of their ideas, that those who adopted these cultural forms would also have adapted their own belief systems to accommodate those of the Celts, and this too would vary from region to region. All of these variables contribute to the difficulty of making a concise summary of Celtic Goddesses, and there is much that we will never know.

Divinities

The primary sources of information that we have about

Celtic divinities – in the form of dedicatory inscriptions, figural sculpture, and Classical accounts – are also the most problematic. It is not until the Roman period that we begin to see a proliferation of images depicting Celtic gods, or find the names of these gods written as dedications on temples or on offertory and curse tablets. By this time, the native divinities had been conflated with those of Rome, creating a Romano-Celtic amalgam which, while useful in giving us insight into the nature of Celtic gods, also by definition represents an adulteration of the original traditions. So while, for example, the association of the Gallic god Taranis with the Roman Jupiter which appears on several inscriptions throughout the Celtic world allows us to use what we know about the Roman king of the gods in order to extrapolate the purview of the lesser-known Taranis – in this case, they are both thunder gods – there is no way of knowing how accurate, or complete, this generalization might be.

The paucity of pre-Roman representations of Celtic divinities tells us that either there was a preference to not create images of their gods, in much the same way their religious teachings were passed on through the oral tradition, or that the images the Celts did create were made from substances which would not have survived into the archaeological record. Indeed, there are some scant examples of what are believed to be votive offerings or divinity images carved into oaken heartwood. These images are very rare, and have primarily been found as *ex voto* deposits in sacred wells and springs both on the continent and in the British Isles. By the time we start seeing images in stone, the gods have already been interwoven with Roman divinities, and so the attendant iconography may not be accurately representative of native tradition.

In his *Gallic Wars*, Julius Caesar gives us a lengthy description of the gods worshiped by the Celtic Gauls; while these divinities have not yet become co-mingled with the Roman gods at the time of his writing, Caesar names them through the filter of his own pantheon, associating them with his own gods based upon their attributes. Unfortunately, he does not record their native names.

They worship as their divinity, Mercury in particular, and have many images of him, and regard him as the inventor of all arts, they consider him the guide of their journeys and marches, and believe him to have great influence over the acquisition of gain and mercantile transactions. Next to him they worship Apollo, and Mars, and Jupiter, and Minerva; respecting these deities, they have for the most part the same belief as other nations: that Apollo averts diseases, that Minerva imparts the invention of manufactures, that Jupiter possesses the sovereignty of the heavenly powers; that Mars presides over wars. To him, when they have determined to engage in battle, they commonly vow those things which they shall take in war (J. Caesar, *The Gallic Wars*, VI, XVII).

Celtic Archaeologist Miranda Green delineates three primary groups of Celtic divinities – those associated with fertility, water, and the sky; of the latter group, gods of the sun and thunder predominate. We can track the frequency and distribution with which divinities are named or depicted on dedicatory inscriptions from the Roman period on; this gives us some information about how popular the veneration of a particular god may have been, as well as how widespread their worship may have become, although Green cautions that this does not tell us the order of importance of these divinities. The more localized distributions may point to tribal divinities or those who were genius loci of a particular location, while more widespread mentions could indicate a more universal Celtic pantheon of sorts. Green notes that the cults of the Mother Goddess – often depicted in triplicate, holding produce and children and ostensibly presiding over fertility – the Sky God, and the horse goddess Epona are the most widespread in the Celtic world. Yet, in general, the Celts seem drawn to venerate their local divinities "in Gaul, over 400 different Celtic god names are recorded, of which 300 occur only once" (Ross, p.147).

There have been several attempts made at organizing this multitude of divinities, and relating them to what we see in the later vernacular literature of the Christianized Celtic lands. Miranda Green and Noemie Beck have engaged specifically, but separately, in attempts to catalog Celtic Goddesses by type and function. Beck's research is more recent, and so will serve as the primary guide for the overview that follows. She identifies five different categories: The Mother Goddesses; Goddesses of Nature and Bounty; Territorial and War Goddesses; Water Goddesses, and Intoxicating Goddesses.

The Mother Goddesses

This is the most ancient group of Goddesses, and the group for which we have a great deal of early material culture, including votive inscriptions and iconography from the Roman Period. It is possible that the worship of the Matres or Matronae as they are variously called is a direct continuation of the earliest veneration of Fertility Goddesses, attested to from the Paleolithic period and onward. The Celtic iteration of the Matronae comes to us from Gaulish culture, and their cultus was popular with Germanic tribes as well as with the Romans, who adapted the practice; it is this Romanization of the worship of the Mothers which resulted in the erection of steles and dedicatory altars to these Goddesses — devotional works which have gifted us with precious information, albeit already influenced by Roman culture.

Usually depicted in groups of three, the seated Matronae typically have baskets of bread or fruit, nursing children, and diapers in their laps. They often wear stylized headdresses, lunulae around their necks, and have associations with trees. Their worship appears to have been widespread, existed as a formal cultus with temples as well as with individual household shrines, and appear to be groupings of divine ancestresses with varying attributes, rather than representing the same three divinities. For example, some of the Matronae are guardians of specific tribes or territories, while others oversee particular functions like fate or aspects of nature.

The Celtic triple Goddess convention may have arisen from the worship of the Matronae, as seen with the Morrigan and Brigid of the Irish. In her triple fate aspect, we may see a precursor to the Germanic Norns, as well as a connection to some of the fairy folk found in Celtic lands; the Welsh called the fae *Bendith y Mamau* – the "Blessings of the Mothers". The single form Matrona has a reflex in the Welsh Modron, and may be related to Mother Goddesses such as Irish Danu and Welsh Don.

Goddesses of Nature and Its Bounty

This is a very wide category which includes Goddesses who are embodiments of the land itself; Goddesses who oversee the riches of the land; and Goddesses who represent specific aspects of nature, such as particular animals, trees, or topographic elements. It is clear that in general, the Earth and its bounties were considered to be under the guardianship of female deities, who often are literally represented in the landscape. In Gaul, we know a few of these divinities from votive inscriptions, such as Litavi, who is a divine embodiment of the Earth; Beck sees resonances of Litavi in Ériu, Banba, and Fótla, Irish Goddesses representing the land and granters of sovereignty over it. The Morrigan, too, was a sovereignty Goddess, and a protector of the land in her martial aspect. One translation of her name is "Great Queen", the same meaning as the Welsh Rhiannon, a sovereignty Goddess with distinct equine characteristics.

The Matronae certainly represent Goddesses connected to the rich abundance of the land, with their nursing babies, fruit, and cornucopiae. The name of the Gaulish Goddess Rosmerta is one of complex etymology, and may possibly mean "The

Great Provider". She was widely worshiped in Gaul, and is often depicted partnered with Mercurius, a Gallo-Roman God who himself has associations with commerce and distribution of wealth.

There are many examples of Goddesses who are the embodiment of specific natural elements. Both Artio ("Bear") and Andarta ("Great Bear") are Goddesses who are connected both iconographically and etymologically to specific animals. Similarly, there are Matronae who are associated with trees, for example: the Baginatiae ("Beech Mother Goddesses"), the Dervonnae ("Oak Mother Goddesses"), and the Eburnicae ("Yew Mother Goddesses"). Goddesses of High Places is the last of these divisions, and includes Goddesses whose names feature the element *Brig-*, which means "The High Ones". These include the British Brigantia (whose name may mean "Hill Fort"), and the Irish Brigid, that triune Goddess holding rulership over poetry, crafts, and healing. In this case, the *bri-* may not mean a literal high place so much as an indication of a "high" or "exalted" deity, for Brigid was greatly revered by the Irish, even into the Christian period.

Territorial and War Goddesses

The Celts were fiercely tribal peoples, and often their Goddesses bore the names of their tribes; alternatively the tribes were named for the Goddesses who protected them. Perhaps the most well-known example of this is Brigantia, the Goddess of the Brigantes, a powerful British tribe. In Gaul, there are many instances of Matronae and Matres dedications which featured by-names that indicated they were being worshiped as the Great Mother ancestresses of the tribe, for example: the Matres Suebae of the Subei tribe, and the Matronae Vanginehae of the Vangiones.

In what can be seen perhaps as an extension of their function as Goddesses of the land, many sovereignty Goddesses also function as protectors of these lands, and have come to feature fierce martial qualities that seem to be in opposition to their more nurturing aspect of providing the abundance of the land. In Ireland, the Goddess Macha ("The Plain") is one of the three Goddesses who comprise the Morrigan, and served independently as the tutelary Goddess of Ulster, whose sacred center was Eamhain Macha. The other aspects of the Morrigan are Babd ("Crow"), and sometimes Nemain, whose name means "Battle Fury".

There are many connections between crows and war, as the carrion birds were a constant presence at battles, and Celt-Iberian tribes had a tradition of exposing the bodies of their dead soldiers to be consumed by crows. Considered messenger birds, they were also looked upon as omens of death, and there appears to be several Goddesses related to these fateful birds, including the Irish Babd. In Gaul, Cathubodua was a war Goddess whose name means "Battle Crow." In Wales, the Goddess Branwen's name means "White or Holy Raven", a bird which is a close relative of the crow. While she is not specifically depicted as a war Goddess in *Y Mabinogi*, a medieval redaction of Welsh mythos believed to have been preserved in the oral tradition from Pagan Celtic times, she does catalyze a war which devastated all of Ireland and all but seven of the British hosts who came to battle. Perhaps Branwen played a more directly martial role in ancient tales.

Another British war Goddess is Andraste ("The Invincible"), to whom the Iceni Queen Boudicca ("Victorious") gave the gift of a hare before battle as she was leading a revolt against Roman invaders in the 1st century, CE. The aforementioned Brigantia is often depicted wearing a helmet and holding a spear, and is a perfect example of a type of Goddess that appears to exist in many iterations across Celtic cultures: a tutelary Goddess of the land, whose name is borne by the tribe living in her territory, and who is a fierce war Goddess who battles to protect her people.

Water Goddesses

The Celts considered water to be sacred. We have evidence of shrines built and offerings deposited at the sources of rivers, we know of many bodies of water that are personified by the Goddesses whose names they bear, have uncovered rich caches of votive offerings that have been placed in lakes and rivers as gifts to the Gods, and ample testimony to belief in the curative powers of the waters of sacred springs and holy wells.

River Goddesses are found all over the Celtic world: In Gaul, Sequina ("To Pour" or "To Stream") is the Goddess of the Seine, and Matrona ("Divine Mother") is Goddess of the river Marne. The Boyne in Ireland is named for the Goddess Bóinn or Bóand, ("White Cow"), and the Shannon River is named for Sinann ("Old Honored One"), a princess who fell into the Well of Seigas as she searched for the hazelnuts of wisdom; she drowned and was reborn as the tutelary Goddess of the river, which now bore her name. In Britain, the river Brent is believed to be named for the Goddess Brigantia, and Sabrina ("Boundary") is the Goddess of the Severn River.

The Celts believed that the Otherworld could be reached through water, either by undertaking a journey by boat across the Ninth Wave of the sea, or through the water itself; because of this, lakes, springs, and rivers were places where votive offerings were given to the Gods in hopes of gaining their blessings, as well as in thanks for blessings and healing received. These latter offerings tend to take the form of the body parts which have been healed. There is a strong connection between water and healing in Celtic traditions, and invariably, it is a Goddess who is both personification of the water and the deity of healing. Perhaps the best example of this is the Goddess Sulis-Minerva, whose Romano-British shrine was built around the thermal springs at Bath. Sulis-Minerva is a syncretic Goddess, a combination of the British Goddess Sulis and the Roman Minerva, in the style of the *Interpretatio Romana* — the conflation of indigenous Gods of conquered peoples with those of the Roman pantheon, although typically the Roman God is named first. In northern Britain, the Goddess Coventina had a thriving cult site at a sacred spring, but there are no direct connections with healing found in the archaeological record. Thermal springs in Gaul were also places of worship for the healing Goddesses Sirona ("Divine Star") and Damona ("Divine Cow").

Intoxicating Goddesses

Unlike the Goddesses already discussed who are intrinsically connected to the natural world, these are deities who are associated with altered states and inebriation, especially concerning the ritual drinking of mead. These altered states were considered a way to enter into the Otherworld as in trance to bring back poetry and prophecy, and so was a form of Imbas or Awen, divine inspiration. Furthermore, the relationship between war Goddesses and Goddesses of inebriation speak to the battle frenzy of the Celtic warriors; the Morrigan, for example, is often depicted inciting men into battle. The name of the Irish Medb means "Mead" or "Intoxicating Goddess", and may also reference her role as a sovereignty Goddess; there appears to be a strong connection between these two functions.

In Gaul, there was a group of Matronae called Comedovae, which either meant "The Ones Who Intoxicate with Mead" or the "Ones Who Rule". Beck writes that these "two etymologies are acceptable, since *med- and *medu- are derived from two homonymic roots, respectively referring to intoxication and sovereignty; notions which were interrelated". They appear to have functioned as healing divinities as well. In Britain, two Goddesses are known who have names associated with inebriation: Latis "Drink (Conveyor)", and Braciaca "Goddess of Beer". There are hints of mead rituals associated with sovereignty rites in Irish literature, and the idea persists that the mead itself was divine, and is sometimes personified by a Goddess.

Conclusion

As this brief overview hopefully makes clear, even though we are working with incomplete information, the Goddesses of the Celts were very complex deities; the roles they played and the attributes they embodied tended to overlap with each other and often lacked clear boundary lines. They generally were concerned with the well-being of their lands, the care and nourishment of the people who lived there, and also served to inspire poetry, prophecy, and healing. While these are not pan-Celtic deities, they are certainly deity types which can be found across Celtic cultural lines, as well as through time as some of these Goddesses turn up as Otherworldy women, fairy queens, and other supernatural characters in the medieval literature of Ireland, Wales, and Brittany. With roots in the distant past, the Goddesses of the Celts are growing strong, reaching their branches out to touch us in the here and now. May they continue to touch and transform those who will come after us.

Jewish
Goddess

Lilith & Eve ~ Laurie Martin-Gardner

"In the beginning, God created the heaven and the earth" (Genesis 1:1). These simple words begin the Judeo-Christian account of the formation of the universe. It is a story that has been told and retold for thousands of years, transcending religion and culture, to become one of the most recognized narratives in the world. Through his word and will alone, God fashions the cosmos, sets into motion the mechanism of time, and fills the empty world with creatures that swim, fly, and walk. From dust, God creates the first man, Adam. To Adam he gives dominion over all living things and places him within the earthly paradise, the Garden of Eden. Later, from Adam's rib, God shapes woman as a companion and helpmate to man. It is that woman, Eve, who will eventually cause the fall of mankind, bringing into the world evil and death.

For millions around the world, the Genesis account is a literal, detailed account of the creation of the world. Some see it as a metaphorical tale to explain the plight of humanity, and yet others see it as no more than a fanciful tale bearing no literal worth at all. Regardless of the lens through which it is read, the story of Adam and Eve is far more profound than many may realize. At face value, it's just one of a multitude of creation stories set down by our ancestors. But delve a bit deeper, and it becomes a profound story of the death of the Mother Goddess and sets into motion attitudes that will prevail throughout the centuries to this very day. And at the heart of the story is not one, but two, women crafted by the very hand of God – Lilith and Eve.

The name of Eve may be a familiar one, but for many, Lilith is virtually unknown. Her name appears only once in the Bible, in the book of Isaiah, and then only in certain early translations. Lilith was born of Mesopotamia, a terrifying she-demon of the wind and night. Lilith first emerges in the epic Sumerian poem *Gilgamesh and the Huluppu-Tree*. In the tale, the goddess Inanna has chosen a specific willow tree to craft a throne from. When she goes to harvest the tree, however, she finds a terrifying trio of creatures has already taken possession of her prized tree: a dragon lies at its base, a zu-bird and her young reside in its branches, and the demoness Lilith resides within the tree itself. Gilgamesh comes to the aid of the goddess and banishes the creatures. Lilith, in this account, flees into the desert.

In Assyria, Lilith was included among the "lilitu", a group of demons that preyed upon sleeping men, pregnant women, and newborn children. In Babylon, she was depicted as the prostitute of the goddess Ishtar. Likewise, she appears in earlier Sumerian tales as the prostitute, or handmaiden, of Inanna who would be sent out to lead men astray.

Regardless of the incarnation she took in the Mesopotamian world, Lilith was always portrayed as a nefarious seductress leading men to evil and stealing the life from women and children. Throughout the ancient world, amulets and inscriptions have been uncovered that attempted to ward off the evil Lilith. Among these are so-called "Lilith bowls". These bowls would be buried inside the house and were believed to be able to trap the demoness should she enter the abode.

So well-known was Lilith as a murderess of children and defiler of men that no explanation of her origins was given in her lone Biblical appearance. She is simply stated as residing in infertile desolation, equating her to a force of chaos and turmoil. She does, however, re-emerge in the collection of ancient texts known as the Dead Sea Scrolls discovered in Qumran in the mid-20th century. The ancient Qumran sect was well versed in demonology and writes of Lilith in the *Song for a Sage*. This piece, possibly used during exorcisms, lists Lilith among "those that strike suddenly, to lead astray the spirit of understanding, and to make desolate the heart".

Although already known among the Jewish people as a powerful demon, Lilith would not receive scholarly interpretation until the compilation of the Talmud. The Talmud, a principal text of Rabbinic Judaism, contains both legal discussions and interpretations of Biblical content. In it, Lilith is described as having long hair and wings, possibly drawing on her earlier incarnations in Babylon. The picture created of Lilith within the Talmud is one of the horrific succubus, a she-demon that has sex with men while they sleep to spawn countless numbers of demonic children. The Talmud goes so far as to warn men to never sleep in a house alone lest Lilith defile him in the night.

For centuries, Lilith haunts the collective imagination of our ancestors as a malevolent force of destruction. She is feared and protected against, and her name is spoken in uneasy whispers. But beginning in the Middle Ages, Lilith will be reborn and introduced as the first wife created for Adam. A wild and indomitable woman, Lilith becomes a darker, more violent figure – the mother of all demons.

The idea that God created an earlier version of woman before Eve comes from Jewish midrashic literature. Midrash, an ancient and important practice within Judaism, is the tradition of making inferences based on Biblical scripture in an attempt to resolve conflicting passages. A careful reading of the book of Genesis reveals two opposing tales of the creation of woman. The first comes in Genesis 1:27 and states, "So God created man in his own image, in the image of God created he him; male and female created he them." In this verse it is implied that man and woman are created at the same time, from the same substance. Yet later, in the second chapter of Genesis, there is a more extensive account of creation that claims man was created first from the dust of the earth and later woman created from the rib of Adam: "And the rib, which the Lord God had taken from man, made he a woman, and brought her unto the man" (Genesis 2:22). The obvious discrepancies between the two creation stories gave rise within the midrashic tradition (and can be found in the Genesis Rabbah) that there must have been an earlier, failed version of woman created before the Biblical Eve.

It wasn't until the 8th-10th centuries that Lilith emerged as the first wife of Adam. The earliest connection between Lilith and the unavailing first woman comes in *The Alphabet of Ben Sira,* largely considered today by scholars as a satirical text containing 22 chapters each corresponding to one of the 22 letters of the Hebrew alphabet. It is in the fifth chapter of *The Alphabet* that Lilith is introduced as the woman created in Genesis 1:27. In this account, Adam and Lilith are created together, equally, from the dust of the earth. But almost as soon as Adam and Lilith had been created, they began to argue. The tension escalates and finally erupts when Adam insists that Lilith take the submissive position during sex, insisting that he was created to be superior to woman. Lilith refuses saying, "We are equal to each other inasmuch as we were both created from the earth." When no resolution can be reached between the two, and neither willing to relent from their position, Lilith utters the Ineffable Name of God and flies away from the Garden of Eden.

Angry and probably a bit embarrassed, Adam prays to the Creator to bring Lilith back to him. God then sends three angels – Senoy, Sansenoy, and Semangelof – to find Lilith and return her to Adam. The angels find her on the shore of the Red Sea, but she emphatically refuses to return to her suppressor. When threatened with death by the angels, Lilith proclaims that she was created to cause sickness and death in infants. She claims dominion over male babies for 8 days after birth and for 20 days after the birth of a female child. To prevent the angels from slaying her, Lilith swore to them that any child bearing an amulet inscribed with the names of the three angels would be spared. The angels agreed, but cursed Lilith so that every day one hundred of her demonic children would perish.

When God learns that Lilith will not return to the Garden, he causes a deep sleep to come over Adam. While he sleeps, God removes a rib from Adam and fashions the woman from Genesis 2:22, Eve. She is presented to Adam and he says in Genesis 2:23 "this is now bone of my bones, and flesh of my flesh".

The rest of the story is undoubtedly familiar to most – the serpent convinces Eve to eat of the forbidden fruit of The Tree of Knowledge which she in turn shares with her husband. Eating the fruit reveals to Adam and Eve their own nakedness, and they are ashamed and hide from God. When confronted, Adam blames the transgression on Eve who in turn blames it on the serpent. In the end, all three are cursed and mankind falls from its once preeminent place in paradise.

In some traditions, after the fall, Adam separates from Eve for a time. Spying him alone, Lilith falls upon Adam as he sleeps, and he unknowingly sires a legion of demonic offspring with her. Lilith again becomes the succubus, birthing a race of children destined to die in multitudes every single day. And because she fled the Garden before the fall, she remains untouched by death forever preying on the "sons of Adam". Afterward, Lilith will become the consort of Samael, or Satan. Eventually, she will be all but forgotten until reclaimed by modern feminists for her strength and unwavering independence.

Comparing the Judeo-Christian creation story with other contemporary stories shows a distinct shift beginning to take place. No longer did life spring from the Mother Goddess. Instead, a Father God reigns supreme without a feminine balance. In this way, the story of the Garden of Eden and the Fall of Man can be seen as a pivotal moment where suppression of the divine feminine begins to occur.

Before the Judeo-Christian reimagining of the creation of the cosmos, the great Mother Goddess was venerated throughout the ancient world. Her form often changed between cultures, but her essence remained the same. From her all life sprang from a balanced connection to the god. When it was time for a creature to die, it was returned to the Mother Goddess where it would find renewed life once again. This ever flowing circle of birth, death, and rebirth was evident to our ancient ancestors as they witnessed it each year with the passing of the seasons.

In Genesis, the god Yahweh strips the duty of birth away from the Mother Goddess, becoming the sole source of creation. All things now come from God and God alone. From the earth, the very body of the Mother Goddess, he creates man. Man is given dominion over earth and all living creatures. The great Mother Goddess is reduced to nothing more than a servant to mortal man, to be manipulated and used according to his will. Putting aside for a moment the tale of Lilith and the first wife, Eve is then created from the rib of Adam in an act contrary to the natural order of life. She is not born of a mother, but created out of man. The tree of life, once a symbol of the goddess herself, becomes the Tree of Knowledge and the catalyst of the fall of humanity. For the Yahwist writers of the Bible, the mother goddess would bring about her own demise.

When before death was seen as a natural transformation, once Eve eats of the forbidden fruit death becomes a finality. No longer is it a transitory state linking birth to rebirth. Death becomes a barren void, a punishment that did not exist before Eve. In this way, the Mother Goddess is defeated. Woman has become the harbinger of death whose life depends solely on the will of God. In cursing Adam and Eve, Yahweh also curses the earth itself. No longer will humanity dwell in the plush, fertile grounds of Eden. Instead, they will be forced to toil and suffer in the dry dust that was once the Mother herself.

For the early Judeo-Christians, one point was decidedly clear – woman was the cause of all evil in the world. But, how could she not be? In the minds of these early adherents, woman was flawed from the moment of her creation. Putting aside the story of Lilith, woman was secondary and created from inferior materials. She was weaker, subject to her husband's will as well as to the will of God. It is that weakness that allowed the serpent (another ancient symbol of the goddess usurped and distorted by the Yahwist writers) to tempt Eve into sin.

In the Old Testament book of Ezekiel it is stated, "The son shall not bear the iniquities of the father, neither shall the father bear the iniquity of the son" (Ezekiel 18:20). And although the meaning of this verse is evident, the same separation of guilt was not afforded to the daughters of Eve. The iniquity of Eve became the justification for the repression of women throughout the Judeo-Christian world. Just as Eve had been created to serve Adam, women were seen as little more than property to their fathers and husbands. They possessed no degree of autonomy as the women of other contemporary cultures enjoyed. Even the sacred act of birth would be ripped away from them as men were believed to be the primary creator of life and the female merely the incubator. The Bible, philosophers, and scholars proclaimed woman's vileness, weakness, and worthlessness. These ideals would become so ingrained into religion and society as a whole that women to this very day struggle to prove their equality and worth to their male counterparts.

In recent decades, as feminism has grown from an idea into a worldwide movement, women have begun to reclaim the power stripped away from their foremothers. The independence and sexual freedom that Lilith was willing to give up paradise for, once viewed as evil and unnatural, is now championed by women seeking to separate themselves from outdated patriarchal attitudes. Eve becomes a symbol for the quiet strength of womankind that can be subdued but not destroyed. Lilith is the woman in the streets championing for equality at the top of her lungs, while Eve is the woman working quietly behind the scenes. Lilith is sexual freedom, and Eve the consummate mother. Together, they represent the whole of femininity.

Modern pagans, both female and male, have also begun to reconnect with Lilith and Eve. For some pagans and occultists,

Lilith represents the "first mother", or sometimes, the dark aspect of the goddess. Eve, as more people delve deeper into her mysteries, has begun to reclaim her position among other great Mother Goddesses such as Isis, Astarte, and Ishtar. As more people attempt to understand and connect with the energies of Lilith and Eve, other associations will undoubtedly emerge to transform our perception of both the individual and womankind as a whole.

Regardless of the multitude of varying (and often contradictory) interpretations of the Judeo-Christian creation story, the figures of Eve and Lilith persevere. Despite the best efforts of many, the Mother Goddess imagery within their stories has not been lost. Instead it has been transformed, molded by countless cultures and the passing of time. It is likely that as the role of women continues to evolve so too will the story of the first females of Genesis. Perhaps as our progenitors, that is their greatest contribution to humanity – the ability to persevere under duress and to rebel against anything that attempts to enslave the spirit.

Asherah ~ Laurie Martin-Gardner

From the depths of history, their names come to us – Isis, Pachamama, Durga, Gaia, Danu, Frigga, and countless others. Powerful goddesses, eliciting adoration (and sometimes trepidation) among their peoples. Each goddess encompasses her own rich mythology and claims her own sacred symbols. Created within the cultural context of the people they represented, each goddess has her own unique traits that set her apart from the others. But a common thread connects them, transcending physical borders and the construct of time. They are the great Mother Goddesses, creatresses of the world. They nurture their people, teach them, and guide them. We see their legacy in historical sites, crumbling papyrus, great temples, and simple altars all around the world. In fact, it would be difficult to find any historical group of people that did not have their own version of the Mother Goddess. She is universal, for our ancestors understood the duality of nature and that all life springs from the feminine.

There is, however, one glaring instance where the Mother Goddess seems to have been omitted, forgotten, or perhaps even lost. Where is the Mother Goddess to balance the Hebrew Father God, Yahweh? On the surface, the answer seems simple – there isn't one. God created all, alone, through his own will and nothing more. No receptacle was needed to birth the world or its inhabitants. The Bible is full of stories where Yahweh either states or proves that he alone is God. But, what if I told you that once there was a Mother Goddess among the Hebrew peoples? One who, for many, was no less than the consort of Yahweh himself.

Her name is Asherah, and she is arguably the most important goddess in the Canaanite pantheon. Her story begins in the ancient port city of Ugarit, in present day Syria. It was there, in

1928, when a farmer ploughing his field accidentally discovered an ancient tomb within a forgotten necropolis. Archaeologists began excavations and discovered a city whose beginnings date back as far as 6000 BCE. The discovery yielded a treasure trove of cuneiform tablets, most dating to around 1200 BCE, containing the rich mythology of the Ugaritic people. It was these tablets that would re-introduce a lost goddess to the modern world.

In Ugaritic literature she was known as Athirat, lady of the sea, and was married to the great god El. The clay tablets tell us that she was the "creatress of the gods" giving birth to a pantheon of children including the Biblical antagonist, Ba'al. She was to her people, the great Mother Goddess. She played the role of wet nurse to gods and worthy mortals alike. Often she was seen as an intermediary, petitioning her husband on the behalf of god or man. She was exalted for her wisdom and sought for her gifts of foresight. There is evidence that she was also revered as a fertility goddess, reigning over pregnancy and childbirth. When the earliest Israelites arrived in the region, worship of Athirat was already well established. In her, the Israelites recognized a nurturing mother, someone that could be called upon to ensure a bountiful crop or an easy birth. So, as it has happened countless times before and after, Athirat was adopted by the early Israelites and the goddess Asherah was born.

Evidence suggests that among the rural Israelite peoples, Asherah was being venerated as early as the twelfth century BCE. It's important to note before continuing that there were often distinct variations in the manner of worship among the common folk in the fields and the ruling class in the temples. Because there was no central authority, the details of worship rested in the hands of local leaders. And although all doctrine was derived through the Bible, interpretations of that doctrine often greatly varied from community to community.

At this point, some of you may be saying "but wait a minute, Judaism is monotheistic". And you would be absolutely correct. Modern Judaism, and the other religions that sprang from it, are inherently monotheistic. There is, according to the adherents of these religions, one god and only one god. But the roots of Judaism are planted firmly in a region and time when polytheism was the norm. Ancient man looked to the heavens and believed that if there was a father god there must also be a mother goddess. How exactly Asherah was chosen to become an Israelite goddess has been lost to us, but we can find her influence in physical artifacts and within the sacred scriptures of the Hebrew Bible itself.

Before delving in to the Biblical accounts of Asherah worship, a quick explanation of terms is needed. In the Bible, there are numerous accounts of *asherah* (note the lowercase 'a'). Most scholars believe that this asherah denotes a cultic object used in worship of the goddess. These objects typically took the form of a stylized tree carved from wood that would be erected by an altar. The tree symbolism dates back to the earliest Canaanite incarnation of Athirat who was often portrayed with or as the Tree of Life. Whether the Biblical passages denote the goddess or the object is debatable in many instances, but it seems obvious to scholars and laymen alike that one does not exist without the other. In short, there is no asherah without the goddess Asherah.

In the Book of Judges in the Old Testament, the story of Gideon brings us an early glimpse into the worship of Asherah among the early Hebrews. Gideon's father, Joash, was a priest of both Asherah and Ba'al. (Throughout the Biblical references of Asherah, we often find her paired with Ba'al – who at some point supplanted his father, El, for superiority.) Gideon does not approve of the worship of any god but the One True God of Israel and attempts to quell the worship of Asherah and Ba'al by destroying the altars and cutting down the asherah. Unfortunately for him, Gideon has vastly underestimated the dedication of the people of Ofra to the goddess and Ba'al. They call for his death, and he is saved only by his father's position as priest and chieftain.

For generations, statues of the goddess stood undisturbed in rural sanctuaries throughout the region. She would be introduced to the ruling elite and people of Jerusalem by none other than King Solomon (970-931 BCE). Through the Bible we know that Solomon had a plethora of foreign wives – a thousand of them actually – and was often accused of worshiping the various deities that his wives brought with them. Among those was Asherah, "the Goddess of the Sidonians". And while many Israelites condemned Solomon for his idol worship, there seems to have been no violent objection to the goddess as there had been in Gideon's time. Rehoboam, Solomon's son and successor, would take Asherah worship in Jerusalem one step further and introduce her into the Temple itself.

When Israel split into two separate kingdoms (Israel in the north and Judah in the south) during the reign of Rehoboam, the worship of Asherah remained. In the kingdom of Israel, Asherah was introduced to the royal court in Samaria by Jezebel, wife of King Ahab (873-852 BCE). Jezebel was the daughter of the King of Sidon where Asherah worship was at least five centuries old. To please his wife, Ahab erected an asherah as well as an altar to Ba'al.

It was during the reign of Ahab and Jezebel in Israel when one very important event took place. The Biblical prophet Elijah, displeased with the worship of "false gods", challenged the prophets of Ba'al and Asherah to a rain-making contest on Mount Carmel. Four hundred and fifty prophets of Ba'al and four hundred prophets of Asherah are said to have joined Elijah in this demonstration of godly powers. According to the story, when the prophets of Ba'al fail to call down the power of their god, Elijah calls out to Yahweh. Yahweh answers immediately, setting fire to the altar and proving that he is the one true god. The prophets of Ba'al are then seized and slaughtered on the banks of the River Kishon. But what of the prophets of Asherah?

There is no mention made as to their fate, and they do not seem to do any more than witness the battle between the prophets of Ba'al and Elijah. Ba'al was undoubtedly seen by Elijah and the Yahwists as dangerous and in need of subduing. The cult of Asherah, in contrast, seems to have been at the very least tolerated. Some scholars go so far as to say that the worship of Asherah was seen as a necessary complement to the worship of Yahweh.

The Book of Kings states that at the reign of Joahaz (814-798 BCE), the statue of Asherah still stood in Samaria. The two rulers directly before Joahaz, Joram and Johu, had both worked diligently to remove all traces of the cult of Ba'al from Israel. But yet, the veneration of Asherah was left virtually untouched again. It is recorded that "they set up pillars and asherahs for themselves upon every high hill and under every leafy tree, and burnt incense there, on all the high places". Asherah would reign as the supreme Hebrew goddess right until the end of the Israelite monarchy, even surviving the Assyrian invasion. It would not be until the reign of the great reformist King Joshiah of Judah that the last asherah in Israel would be desecrated.

In Judah, Asherah again proved her tenacity and the dedication of her adherents. It was during the reign of Rehoboam, son of Solomon, that Asherah was introduced into the Temple itself. Urged on by his wife, Maacah, Rehoboam installed an asherah next to the altar to Yahweh. There it would remain until Asa (908-867 BCE), encouraged by the prophet Azariah, instituted religious reform for the first time in the Judean kingdom. It is said that Asa cut down and removed the asherahs and burnt them in the Kidron Valley. Interestingly enough, Asa's son Jehoshafat also worked to remove the asherahs from Judah during his reign from 870-846 BCE. This implies that one of two things occurred: either Asa was unsuccessful in removing all of the asherahs or the asherahs re-emerged as quickly as Asa destroyed them.

After the death of Jehoshafat, Joash (836-798 BCE) ascended

the throne of Judah. And although he undertook a massive restoration of the Temple, he also reinstalled the statue of Asherah within the Temple. It would remain in its place next to the altar of Yahweh until the reign of Hezekiah in 727-698 BCE. As soon as Hezekiah died however, his son and heir Manasseh (698-642 BCE) rebuilt the altars to both Asherah and Ba'al. Later King Joshiah, who had destroyed the worship of Asherah in Israel, would order the removal of all asherahs in the kingdom of Judah as well. He also set down the law that no asherah, and indeed no tree at all, should be planted next to the altar of Yahweh unless it invite the wrath of God. But Joshiah's efforts were not as effective in Judah as they had been in Israel. Upon his death, the cults of Asherah and Ba'al sprang up again throughout the countryside. They would persist until the destruction of Jerusalem by Nebuchadnezzar in 586 BCE. For 236 of the 370 years that the Temple of Solomon endured, the statue of Asherah stood equal to the altar of Yahweh.

Why was the cult of Asherah able to survive almost every attempt to quell her dominance? Archaeological evidence clearly demonstrates her importance among the common Hebrew people. Hundreds of small votive figurines of the goddess have been found throughout the region. But was her perseverance due solely to her popularity among the masses? Many scholars now believe they know the answer to that question. Asherah was not merely a great Canaanite mother goddess adopted by the Israelites. Instead she was the consort of Yahweh himself.

Some of the evidence pointing to Asherah as the consort of God is, admittedly, circumstantial. To many researchers, the presence of the asherah next to the altar of the Hebrew God is an obvious nod to the idea that the goddess was the wife of Yahweh. This would explain why Yahwist reformers would often overlook the presence of the Asherah cults and why she was allowed to be portrayed as an equal partner to Yahweh within the Temple. How this connection was made among the people is questionable, but it may harken back to the early Canaan beliefs from which Asherah, and even Yahweh, sprang. Much of the mythology and symbolism of the god El, the original husband of Asherah, was dissolved into and mixed with the concept of Yahweh. And although it would have been quite blasphemous to proclaim among the ancient Israelites, Yahweh also absorbed certain aspects of Ba'al as well. Therefore it is a logical conclusion that El's consort and Ba'al's mother would also be claimed by Yahweh.

However, it was a series of discoveries in the mid-1970s and early 80s that would strengthen the claim that Asherah was the consort of Yahweh. One of the most interesting of these came from the site of Kuntillat Arjud in the northeast Sinai. A large *pithoi*, or storage jar, was discovered at the site carrying an intriguing inscription that read in part "may you be blessed by Yahweh and by his Asherah". Elsewhere in the same site, another inscription reads, "I have blessed you by Yahweh ... and his Asherah." At a separate site at Khirbet al-Qom, yet another inscription reads, "Blessed be Uriah by Yahweh and by his Asherah." These inscriptions confirm that Asherah was intimately connected to Yahweh in the minds and hearts of the Hebrew people. As more evidence is unearthed, it becomes apparent that the veneration of Asherah as the wife of God was an important aspect of worship throughout Israel and Judah. It is most likely this connection that allowed the cult of Asherah to withstand six centuries of attempted subjugation.

In light of Asherah's obvious and enduring importance, how is it that she was lost for so long? Her name appears forty times in the Bible, but not at all in the King James version that so many are accustomed to. By the time of James, she had been demoted to no more than a grove of trees. Even the feminine aspect of her name was stripped away and replaced with the masculine *asherim*. Much of this destruction of the goddess began with the Deuteronomist who wrote and rewrote sections of the Bible in the 7th century BCE. It was paramount to the Deuteronomist that all aspects of goddess worship be eliminated so that Yahweh alone would reign supreme. Women were routinely dismissed as unworthy and evil, nothing more than mere property to their fathers and husbands. The Asherah statues were burnt, and many of her worshipers were sacrificed, by the will of the same God whose altar she had once graced. By equating her to the blasphemous Ba'al, she was declared an abomination and her exaltation outlawed. Over time, her name would be buried so deeply that it would be all but forgotten, lost among a list of pagan goddesses decried by the very people she once championed.

But, just as she had proven again and again in the distant past, Asherah is not an easy goddess to defeat. With her resurgence she has found a home in a time that barely resembles the one in which she was born. Within the modern day country of Israel, a small but growing community is honoring the worship of ancient Semitic deities, including Asherah. In modern pagan groups, Asherah has begun to reclaim her place among the ancient and powerful Mother Goddesses. Progressive Jewish adherents are delving into their history and rediscovering the sacred mother of their people. Like all good mothers, Asherah welcomes her children both new and old, with open arms. This chapter of her story has just begun, but it will undoubtedly continue to evolve as more people connect with and search for the Hebrew goddess.

Sophia and Wisdom Literature
~ Mabh Savage

I was there when he set the heavens in place,
when he marked out the horizon on the face of the deep,
when he established the clouds above
and fixed securely the fountains of the deep,
when he gave the sea its boundary
so the waters would not overstep his command,
and when he marked out the foundations of the earth.
Then I was constantly at his side.
Proverbs 8: 27-30

Hagia Sophia: Holy Wisdom. The Greek words name a Goddess who is the embodiment of the concept of Wisdom; knowledge tempered by good judgment and good sense. The seven sapiential books from the Hebrew Bible that deal with Wisdom (Job, Psalms, Proverbs, Ecclesiastes, Wisdom of Solomon, Song of Solomon and Sirach), and the quest for such, are littered with references to Wisdom not only as a person, but most definitely as a woman. Wisdom is a *She*, just as definitely as Yod-Hei-Vav-Hei, or Yahweh, the figure of God, is absolutely *He*.

Feminist historian and writer Max Dashu convincingly conflates Sophia with Khokhmah (or Hokmah, or Chokmah), an ancient Hebrew feminine noun for Wisdom and an aspect of the Pillar of Mercy in the Kabbalistic Tree of Life. Just as Sophia is seen as an aspect of the Holy Spirit, Khokmah was also an 'emanation of God', (*Streams of Wisdom, Dashu, 2000)*, and was possibly seen as a partner of God. Wisdom can also be seen as part of *Shekhinah*, which in Judaism means the feeling of the presence of God; God's presence on Earth. Shekhinah is another feminine Hebrew word; another tantalizing scrap of evidence that these aspects of a presumed male God, are actually pieces of a divine feminine that longs to be brought into the light. Rabbi Jill Hammer, director of Tel Shemesh, sees Shekhinah as the Divine that resides within the world, a feminine image of 'the inner glory of existence' which accompanies and complements the transcendent male God of Jewish tradition.

The balance between male and female is notable in most holy writings for its absence, yet in the Proverbs we are taught that a man should 'Hear, son, the instruction of thy father, and reject not the rules of thy mother', a clear mandate that honor should be given to both parents. In the same way, more and more people are giving credence to the idea that the divine is a balance of both masculinity and femininity, even within the Bible, the Torah and the other Abrahamic writings that have traditionally been seen as the sole throne of the divine male. If the son must accept the ultimate authority of both mother and father, surely those who are devotees of these religions must accept the ultimate truth of a mother and a father presence; a God and a Goddess, or at the very least an aspect of both male and female within the Godhead.

Jung explored the idea of the Holy Trinity becoming a 'Quaternity', with a feminine aspect completing the four aspects of the Godhead. More recently, a more balanced Godhead has been suggested by some researchers and followers of Sophia (such as Katia Romanoff, co-founder of Esoteric Interfaith Church) as Father, Son, Mother and Daughter. This Quaternity leaves out the Holy Spirit, so perhaps this could be included as a genderless addition, completing a perfectly balanced Quinternity; a Godhead for a new age, where the creative power of Yahweh and the Wisdom of Sophia perfectly complement each other.

In the 13th century, in the face of anti-rationalist behavior, philosopher Shem-Tov ibn Falaquera devoted himself to restoring the harmony of the Torah and Sophia; to the joining of religion and secular wisdom; even the word 'philosopher' means 'the love of Sophia', literally the love of Wisdom. Throughout the ages rationalists and philosophers such as Falaquera have strived to unite theology with reason; to bring to life the Wisdom held within the Holy Writings.

Wisdom in Abrahamic literature often deals with real life, everyday occurrences. It is how to deal with politics, money, household matters, justice in the courts and the rewards for following a righteous and wise path are full storehouses and peace. It is a very grounded part of the religion, and this is probably why it resonates so deeply with so many people, from all walks of life. It is interesting indeed, that where we find the most, real, most relatable parts of religious doctrine we find the feminine divine, and ultimately the first steps towards balance. That is not to say that there is no sense of patriarchy in the translations we have of the Books of Wisdom; far from it. Proverbs is entirely a monologue from father to son, yet within these instructions we gain a sense of the reverence for the deity that *is* Wisdom; that is Sophia herself.

One of the greatest senses I gain from the Wisdom Writings is that Sophia is almost the foil to God's power. He is this amazing, creative force, who brought the world into being from seemingly nothing, and she is like a guiding hand, calming and focusing, driving the energy in the direction it needs to go. This does not always mean she is kind; if she decides to focus God's, or her energy to destroy, then whatever is in her path *will* be decimated, if it is the righteous thing to do. Wisdom does not mean *nice* and it is not necessarily associated with unconditional love, an aspect of God that tends to revolve more around Christ and Mary. Sophia was there at the beginning; she was in the firmament, the foundations of the earth itself. She felt the first mountains groan to the skies and tasted the first droplet of water. She is, in a way, nature itself, all knowing, yet this is not the extent of her being. She is full of knowledge, but able to discern what is true, what is right and what the correct path is to follow, and she allows us the ability to do the same.

Robert Powell, co-founder of the Sophia Foundation of North America, asks the question 'Is divine wisdom simply an attribute of God?' Looking at the evidence, in his lecture *Sophia and the Rose of the World*, Powell decides that Sophia is indeed a separate being; a powerful, divine feminine being. From the lecture:

...in the Russian Orthodox Church there lives a devotion to Sophia. It is not immediately apparent how this came about. One can see from the various Sophia icons from the Russian tradition that all of them show Sophia as a majestic divine feminine being who is raying out wisdom. Above her is Christ, so she is clearly not the same as Christ. To her right is the Virgin Mary, so she is clearly not the same as the Virgin Mary. To her left is John the Baptist.

Powell is emphasizing the point that many who follow Christian or Jewish traditions, also take Sophia's existence for granted. They accept readily that there is a feminine aspect to the divine and that while Sophia is not 'God', not the creator himself, neither is she anything as simple as a mere attribute of His omnipotence. She exists apart from all other divine beings, the home and heart of Wisdom, shedding her own magnificent light upon the world.

One of the proponents of Sophiology generally, but particularly in Russia, was philosopher Vladimir Solovyov (1853-1900), who had several encounters with Sophia as an entity, and taught that she was the merciful, unifying feminine wisdom of God. Like Dashu and Hammer, he also compared her to Shekhinah, and describes her as 'God's breath', offering intuition and creativity. Despite describing her as part of God, when he experienced her first-hand, he described a radiant feminine being in blue light, and knew she was a being in her own right.

In Sirach, another Wisdom writing from the Hebrew Bible, Wisdom is once again referred to as 'she', and also as something created by God; not a part of him, not an aspect, but a being created for the benefit of mankind:

> Sirach 1: 9 He created her, and saw her, and numbered her, and poured her out upon all his works.
> 10 She is with all flesh according to his gift, and he hath given her to them that love him.

Also:

> Sirach 4: 11 Wisdom exalteth her children, and layeth hold of them that seek her.
> 12 He that loveth her loveth life; and they that seek to her early shall be filled with joy.
> 13 He that holdeth her fast shall inherit glory; and wheresoever she entereth, the Lord will bless.
> 14 They that serve her shall minister to the Holy One: and them that love her the Lord doth love.

Unlike the above section from Proverbs, where Wisdom speaks in the first person, here Wisdom is described in the third person as a being we should allow to enter our lives. In the same way as we are expected to accept God's love, to allow God's spirit to enter us, we are to accept Wisdom into our hearts and minds. In the Book of Wisdom (Wisdom of Solomon), Wisdom is described as a 'loving spirit'; not, and I feel this is crucial, God's loving spirit. In Greek, this would have read that Sophia is a loving spirit. Once we replace the word wisdom with Sophia, it becomes clearer and clearer that the Holy books are speaking of a divine being in her own right.

Further into the Book of Wisdom, we learn that:

> Wisdom 7: 22 As for wisdom, what she is, and how she came up, I will tell you, and will not hide mysteries from you: but will seek her out from the beginning of her nativity, and

bring the knowledge of her into light, and will not pass over the truth.

This sounds like the beginnings of a great origin story, and why would a mere aspect of an all-powerful God need its own, separate mythos? Solomon tells us that he prayed to God yet it was Wisdom that came to him, not the almighty.

Wisdom 7: 8 I preferred her before scepters and thrones, and esteemed riches nothing in comparison of her.
9 Neither compared I unto her any precious stone, because all gold in respect of her is as a little sand, and silver shall be counted as clay before her.
10 I loved her above health and beauty, and chose to have her instead of light: for the light that cometh from her never goeth out.
11 All good things together came to me with her, and innumerable riches in her hands.
12 And I rejoiced in them all, because wisdom goeth before them: and I knew not that she was the mother of them.

Even if we are to see Wisdom as an aspect of God, or even a segment of the Godhead, such as the Holy Spirit, there can be no denying that these tales purposefully and intentionally state again and again that this powerful and awe-inspiring being is female. Solomon worshipped Sophia above all things, telling us two things; firstly, he saw Wisdom as the ultimate cardinal virtue, more important than all the others, possibly the root of all the others. Secondly, he saw Sophia as his Goddess; his deity, his tutelary being. It is no wonder then, that so many Jews and Christians today still see the divinity within Sophia, and accept her place within the Abrahamic religions as a source of light, hope and peace.

It's an exciting time for devotees of Sophia, and also for those followers of the Abrahamic religions who are overwhelmed by the patriarchal overtones; who long for balance, and an understanding of the divine feminine. Public speakers like Katia Romanoff travel globally spreading the word of Sophia and her cohorts, giving presentations with titles such as 'God has a wife!' and 'Encountering Mary Magdalene', where she explores the idea of a new Holy Trinity, of Mary Mother of God, Mary Magdalene and Sophia; Mother, Daughter and the Holy Soul. Sophiology is a well-recognized field of theology *and* thealogy now, although considered heretical still by some branches of the church. Romanoff points out that another attraction of Sophia, particularly to women, is that She provides women with 'an image of female power that is not based solely on reproduction and mothering but on another aspect of the feminine archetype rarely discussed: the intelligence and cosmic power of the life force' (*Sophia: Exile and Return*).

In America, the Colorado based Sophia Foundation (mentioned briefly above) seeks to 'cultivate a deeper understanding of Divine Wisdom integrating philosophy, religion, science and the arts'. This is something that seems to flow throughout Sophiology; the deep urge to understand all aspects of the world and the divine, using all the tools at our fingertips. Not just the Holy words of the Alexandrian Jews who brought us the Wisdom writings, but the technology and science now available to us, our ability to think and reason, our intrinsic divinity, plus our own imaginations and creative instincts, surely divine gifts themselves. When we write about Sophia, when we craft a poem, or a picture, or paint an image from a Wisdom meditation, perhaps Sophia speaks through us, letting herself be known in the illumination of reason and enlightenment.

Sophia is a Greek word, and it was Alexandrian Jews that brought her to life, in the Greek translations of the Books of Wisdom that are so readily available in English today. When we read the word 'Wisdom', we must take note of the reverence given to the word, of how deeply the idea is personified. We must highlight the use of the female pronoun, and realize that these Jewish scholars, (allegedly all seventy-two of them) were not discussing an abstract concept, but a divine presence that was most assuredly feminine. Wisdom *is* Sophia; and Sophia is most assuredly a Goddess; a divine being that wishes to be taken into our own spirit and held Holy. Even if you can't accept her as a Goddess in her own right, she is, then, most assuredly a deeply intrinsic aspect, perhaps the Holy Spirit, of the one true God. She may be or have been known as Khokhmah, Shekhinah, or even Asherah, but her divine aspect is her name, and as such she is a beautiful and awe-inspiring Goddess to follow.

When we reach for the Bible or the Torah, the Books of Wisdom or the Writings, we reach for aid, for help; for understanding. For help with our day to day problems, no matter how big or small, we are attempting to apprehend the words of some of the greatest philosophers and theologians, who strove to explain to us the reality of Divinity as they understood it. We are consciously falling into the past, into the divine, and into the arms of the great Lady of Wisdom; Sophia, who teaches us that power is nothing without justice and compassion. In our currently conflicted and hurting world, this is a lesson that seems more and more important every day. In the words of the Sophia Foundation, 'It is Sophia whom we seek as we strive to bring beauty, love, wisdom, justice and peace into our dear world.' A worthy quest indeed.

Mystery
Goddess

Isis: Goddess of a Thousand Names
~ Robin Herne

One of the best known deities of the Egyptian pantheon, devotion to this goddess spread throughout the Roman Empire following their domination of Egypt. The exact pronunciation of the Ancient Egyptian language is unknown, though linguists draw heavily on Coptic for guidance as this is a direct descendant of that language group. Feminine names end in a *t* sound, leading to the likelihood that this deity was known to her own original people as Iset or Aset. For the purposes of this chapter, the form Aset will be used from this point onwards.

A common theme in Egyptian love poetry is to refer to one's husband as brother and wife as sister. This is an expression of intimacy, and should not be viewed as a sign of incestuous inbreeding! Aset is married to her own brother Asur (called Osiris by the Greeks), and whilst this actually is incest it is better understood through the lens of their being twin souls, two sides of the same coin. In the origin story attributed to Aset, she and her husband-brother are the offspring (along with two other siblings) of Father Earth, Qeb, and Mother Sky, Nut. Western mythologies are more inclined to speak of land and sky as gendered the other way round, but Egyptian religion views many things in its own very distinct way.

Aset and Asur are, in many ways, templates for the royal court that was the heart of Egyptian society. One of the central myths describes Asir as a world traveler, bringing the skills of agriculture, metalwork, and so forth alongside more abstract concepts of culture and law to various parts of the world. Many imperialist cultures regard themselves as the civilizing agents of the world, and Egypt was no exception to this. Whilst Asur was off polishing the rough diamond of human society, Aset remained upon the throne – indeed, the hieroglyphs for her name represent the sovereign power of the royal seat. In this respect Egyptian culture does echo concepts found in the west, such as amongst the Celtic cultures where the force of sovereignty that determines the right of mortal leadership is the goddess of the land. A Mexican proverb tells us that a house does not rest upon the ground, but upon a woman (the matriarch of the family) and similar sentiments may be found elsewhere in the world too. Aset is not simply a passive notion of authority; she actively rules the land whilst her husband is traveling. Whilst Egypt was not a feminist paradise, women held many influential roles in society – including within the royal court – and rights or property ownership, divorce, and so forth. Whilst the majority of pharaohs were male, there were numerous powerful female rulers, not to mention the larger number of royal women who acted as the power behind the throne, or as default rulers in cases where their husbands were less than useful.

On one of his visits home, a great feast is laid on for the return of the divine pharaoh, the netjeru (gods) flock to attend and present him with various gifts. One of the gift-bringers is Asur's own brother, the flame haired Setekh who comes bearing an ornately carved and painted chest. Asur is invited to try it out for size (it is, of course, a perfect fit for his reclining body) whereupon the lid is slammed shut and sealed whilst the desert deity's loyal 72 shemsu (followers) subdue the royal court. The sarcophagus is thrown into the Nile where Asur drowns – whilst it is possible he suffocates in an airtight chest, the Memphite Theology inscribed on the Shabaka Stone explicitly states death by drowning. Aset, who has fled the court when her brother and the murderer of her husband seize dominion over the realm, begins the quest to find where the chest has washed up so that she can begin working her magic. A traditional interpretation of the Nile flood (which used to take place during the summer) was that it was caused by the shed tears of Aset as she searched for her brother's corpse.

Aset's magical power stems in no small part from an event accounted for in a short myth wherein she tricks the falcon-headed Re – original pharaoh of the netjeru. Egyptian beliefs about magic depend on the concept of heka and ren. Heka is a spoken (or, rather, sung) spell using renu, as well as being the name of the deity that embodies and regulates the notion of magical force. The renu are the sacred names of things. The Egyptians believed that all living beings (and parts of beings) had a True Name, which could be conceived of as the sound of their soul. This understanding exists alongside the belief that the human (and probably most other creatures too) have nine functioning parts, of which the flesh-and-blood body is but one. At death the nine constituent parts break up and each faces a different fate. One of the parts is the ren. To drop the authorial fourth wall for a moment, we could reflect that the body – when it isn't duly mummified – will eventually rot away and become food for worms. The constituents that make us who we are, including the parts understood by the Egyptians, only temporarily belong to us. The force which binds them all together, which makes them into each unique person for a few short years, is that name, that ren. To be poetic, the ren is the song of each being in existence and together we compose the vast and unending song of creation. One of the mystical tasks within Kemeticism, as the religion of Egypt is often termed these days, is to find one's own ren and sing it properly and passionately.

Returning to that short myth, in the beginning Re sang all living beings into existence. As each ren was spoken, that creature appeared. To know the secret name of a creature is to have power over it. Aset, desiring to extend her influence over the world, spat on the soil and made enough mud to shape a serpent and then sing its name into it – thus bringing the snake to life in a way that is also echoed in the stories of the potter-god Ptah. The reptile slithered off and bit Re in the ankle. As the poison coursed through his body, agony burning him up,

Re realized that he did not know the name of the snake and so could do nothing to halt the spread of the venom. Begging for help, Aset leapt out from hiding and offered to cure the poison if only Re would tell her his secret ren (Re being but a title, not the name of his soul – as, indeed, Aset is a title and not the goddess's ren... the Egyptians were as cagey about their real names as Doctor Who is and for pretty much the same reason). This he did, whereupon Aset dispelled the venom and acquired the title of Weret-hekau in the process (meaning 'She who is Great in Magical Spells'). By learning the name of Re she came to learn the names of all the many creatures and beings that he created, and so was able to influence those whose names she knew. Within this culture, knowledge really is power.

Aset knew her husband's true name and so was intent on using this knowledge to restore him to life. The story of her search for the corpse is a long one, and an interesting element of it is her choice of companion and guardian on the journey – seven giant golden scorpions. A beast sacred to the goddess, these ancient arachnids date back to the Silurian Era and were also considered manifestations of the goddess Serket.

Eventually Aset tracks the sarcophagus to the Canaanite or Phoenician city of Gebal (called Byblos in Greek renditions of the story), which is located in modern day Lebanon. There she learns that the chest has become entangle by the roots of an ancient holy tree and drawn up in its trunk. Plutarch describes this as an Erica tree, a member of the Ericaceae family more commonly known as the giant heather (they can reach up to 23 feet tall, quite unlike the diminutive heathers we are familiar with in Britain). The king of this city, in a display of regal arrogance that would not be out of place in the 21st century, has ordered the miraculous tree to be chopped down and erected as a pillar in the temple at his palace (a reminder that polytheists can be as monumentally stupid as anyone else). Like countless Greek deities, Aset opts to use a disguise when walking amongst mortals who might not otherwise be able to cope with the experience. She presents herself at the palace in the guise of an old woman and becomes a nursemaid to the royal infant. Days roll past until the time when a suspicious queen, whom Plutarch tells us was called Astarte, Sooses, or Neinanoë, spied on the nurse and saw her holding the baby in the fire. The queen snatched her child out of what she considered harm's way only for Aset to manifest before her, reproving that the flames were making the baby immortal but that the mother's actions had broken her spell and rendered the child mortal once again. Aset takes the wooden pillar back to Egypt where she extracts her husband's corpse from it.

The land of Canaan was, for three centuries from 1580 BCE onwards, under Egyptian rule (and before that, part of the Hyksos and the Amorite empires), and Aset's arrival at Gebal may partly allude to this historical event. The goddess is also present at such historical events as the birth of the Fifth Dynasty kings Userkaf, Sahure, and Neferirkare – where she uses her knowledge of their renu to act as a divine midwife. The story told of her interaction with the mothers of these kings suggests that the renu are fixed prior to birth, because she uses them to call the babies out of their respective wombs (or possibly she is the deity that creates their essence by awarding them each a ren).

The opening of the pillar is far from the end of the story, because Aset's murderous brother Setekh has been spying on her and hacks the corpse into many pieces, hurling them hither and yon. A further saga ensues in which Aset manages to track down thirteen pieces of the corpse – the fourteenth part (the one most men would least want to lose) having been eaten by a fish. Aset is not a goddess to be defeated or outdone, for every problem, she finds a creative solution. Just as her brother invented the sarcophagus, so she now invents mummification in order to bind the various body parts together into a unified whole. The lost member is substituted with an artificial one, usually said to be made of gold (the world's most expensive dildo). Thus restored to a semblance of form, Asur is resurrected by his sister-wife's command of the singing magic. For a brief period they are able to unite and conceive a child, before Asur passes into the west to become lord of the land of the dead.

Along with the child conceived through magic, Heru (Horus to the Greeks), another story described how her sister Neheb-het disguised herself as Aset in order to conceive a child with her own husband, the fratricidal Setekh. If this sounds a little strange, it is because Neheb-het's husband does not wish to have a child with her. Having thus deceived her husband, she falls pregnant with Anpu (the jackal-headed Anubis) and eventually convinces Aset to pass the boy off as her own, so becoming an adoptive mother as well as a biological one.

As may be gathered from the story thus far, Aset is the energetic principal in the saga whilst her consort is passive. Having educated the world, he falls into the role of victim and is totally dependent upon Aset's ingenuity and determination. As with Father Earth and Mother Sky, commonplace western gender dynamics are inverted. As a descendant of Father Earth, Asur's death and restoration can be understood as the agricultural cycle of growth, harvesting, and regrowth. The Egyptians portrayed Asur as green-skinned for this very reason. If Asur is, in part, the crops then Aset is the dedicated farmer who learns ways of preserving seed to replenish the fields at next year's sowing (Setekh, cutting down the green lord, is surely the sickle). Not only is she the wisdom of the farmer in setting aside grain for sowing, but also the very impulse of life that seeks to restore vitality where there is death. One of Setekh's titles is Lord of the Red Land (the desert), and he can be considered as ruler of the realm of bareness and abandon – though he does have a life-giving role as well. By contrast Aset, one of whose symbols is the ankh – the hieroglyph for life – is the vivifying power that transforms parched soil into fertile fields.

The mother of all life, Aset goes into hiding with her newly conceived child and nurtures him for many years before he is of an age to fight his own battles against the uncle who has wrested the throne of Egypt. Aset is not a meek Madonna, but the mother and forger of a warrior who raises her son to avenge his father. In this respect we return to Aset as a template for the role expected of any pharaoh's wife (or female ruler in her own right, as Hatshepsut was). She is a ferocious force that will not be quelled or subdued for long, and always plans for the long term. She guides her son through 80 years of feuding and battling against Setekh.

When the adolescent Heru was sexually exploited by his uncle in a bid to discredit him from ever holding the throne (such being the views of those days, before the more sympathetic treatment of rape victims in our current era), his mother counseled him to use the very evidence of the assault against Setekh. Not one for wasted emotion, Aset does what is necessary to depose her brother and establish her son on the throne of a united Egypt. The previously mentioned Shabaka Stone describes Aset brokering peace between Heru and Setekh once the matter of governance is finalized. Given that the decades-long battle has involved not only attempted sexual violence but rather gruesome acts of physical brutality, modern sensibilities might find the prospect of forming peace improbable or even undesirable. However, Aset is a healer of even the most virulent venom and perhaps one to turn to for help when the level of damage seems beyond the capacity of humans to repair.

After the Romans conquered Egypt they rather fell in love with Aset, or Isis as they preferred to call her. Temples, or Iseums as the Romans called them (Iseion to the Greeks), appeared all over the vast empire – including one on the banks of the Thames, where St Paul's Cathedral now stands. Within these Iseums the religion became a mystery cult. The mystery cult of Isis spread in the Hellenic world some three centuries before the Common Era, where she became more closely allied with Serapis than

Asur/Osiris.

The form of cultus that spread through Greece and its colonies was not entirely Egyptian, but a fusion of Hellenic and Kemetic ideas and practices developed by the priests Manetho and Timotheus under the direction of Ptolemy I. The Greek rulers appointed in the aftermath of Alexander the Macedonian's conquest of Egypt wanted to promote a religion that would draw the best of both cultures together, and Isis became a central force in making this happen.

As it spread through Rome, the devotees were initially all male but this changed until, by the second century of the Common Era they were mostly female. Both Plutarch and Apuleius describe devotees as adopting the Egyptian habits of shaving their heads and dressing in linen. The Aretalogy of Maroneia, written in the first century BCE, describes Isis as the discoverer of the holy books which are known only to the members of the mystery cult. This would seem to be a new introduction within the devotions to this goddess, and no copies of these secret texts are known to survive. Plutarch describes an annual ceremony of the cult of Isis, the *Navigium Isidis* held on 5th March, where a small unmanned boat stocked with offerings was sailed out on the tides and presumably either washed ashore down river or sank. The goddess had become strongly associated with sailors and merchants who made their living via the waterways.

An author called Isidoros, writing around the first century BCE, describes Isis as having countless names, being known under different identities to assorted cultures. The idea of a deity being known under numerous titles is not unique to Isidoros, but it does take off within the mystery cults and is arguably the birth of inclusive monotheism. Professor Garth Fowden and other historians consider it likely, from the style of writing that Isidoros was of Greek descent. Isidoros's view of the goddess reflects a shift from distinctly Egyptian deity to an overarching supreme goddess, a hidden core at the heart of all other goddesses. This manifestation of Isis inspired Helena Blavatsky in 1877 with her rambling book *Isis Unveiled* where the veil of Isis is the natural world and her presence unveiled is the cosmic truth underpinning reality.

It is in this form that she is most widely known today, such as in her role as inspirer of the Fellowship of Isis founded in 1973. One of its founders, Olivia Robertson, died recently leaving a considerable legacy of research, philosophy, and activism behind her. Whilst a fair number of modern pagans turn to Isis in her aspect as Goddess of Mysteries, others devote themselves to Aset, the early Egyptian understanding of that deity. In whatever guise she is understood, her presence has been felt by humanity for many thousands of years, and is liable to go on being felt long into the future.

Eleusinian Mysteries ~ Jennifer Uzzell

In very ancient times, Greece was the source of a group of religious traditions collectively known as 'Mysteries'. These differed from official state religion in a variety of ways. Most obviously, they possessed secret knowledge revealed by the gods only to those who had undergone the 'mysteries' of initiation. This knowledge allowed an intimate and personal relationship with the god or goddess with whom they were associated and secured a favourable afterlife. Of these Mysteries, perhaps the best known is that of the Goddess of grain and agriculture, Demeter, and her daughter Kore (or Persephone) at Eleusis.

The Eleusinian Mysteries were closely tied to a myth best known to us from the Homeric Hymn to Demeter, composed in the Seventh Century BCE. According to the hymn, Kore (meaning 'maiden') was out gathering flowers in the fields with her friends. At this time, there were no seasons and the earth was warm and bountiful all year round and so every type of flower was blooming all year round. Kore was attracted to a particularly beautiful and fragrant narcissus, but as she bent down to pick it the earth split open beneath her and Hades, Lord of the Dead, grabbed her and carried her, screaming, to the underworld to be his wife. The terrified girl struggled and screamed to the sun, the earth and all the gods to save her, but as Hades had abducted her with the permission of his brother Zeus, king of the gods, none dared come to her aid. Her mother, Demeter, Lady of the fertile fields and the harvest, realised that something was terribly wrong. For nine days, she wandered all over the earth carrying a burning torch, calling desperately for Kore, and begging everyone she met, god and mortal for news of her. Hecate, the triple headed goddess of crossroads went to Demeter and told her that she had seen Kore carried away but had not seen who had been responsible. Without a word

Demeter rushed to Helios, the sun god who sees all, still carrying her blazing torch and accompanied by Hecate. Demeter pleaded with Helios to tell her what he knew and he told Demeter that she should now cease to be worried and sad since Kore had been given as a bride to Hades by Zeus. She was safe and would be honoured by Hades, who would not make a bad son in law. He was a great god since, in time, all living things honoured him. Demeter, however, was not consoled, rather she was filled with rage at the treachery of her brother, Zeus. She vowed that she would never again set foot in Olympus, the abode of the gods, until she was once again united with her daughter.

Demeter disguised herself as an old woman named Demos, wrapped in a dark cloak and veiled, and set off wandering in the world of mortals. As she rested by a well at Kallichorn, the daughters of Keleos, ruler of the city of Eleusis came to collect water. They spoke to her respectfully, asking why she had not come into the city, where she would be kindly treated. Demeter claimed that she had come from Crete and had escaped from pirates who hoped to sell her as a slave. She accepted the girls' invitation to enter their household as nurse to their infant brother Demophon. When she entered the house, it was filled with divine radiance and Metaneira, the boy's mother, was filled with awe and wonder. She stood up to offer her chair to the strange guest, but Demeter cast down her eyes and said nothing. One of the household servants, a girl called Iambe, realised that she did not desire a grand seat and set up for her a folding stool covered with a fleece. And so she sat, silent and veiled, refusing to speak or eat. Iambe made many jokes and eventually persuaded Demeter to smile. Metaneira offered her fine red wine but she refused this and asked instead for a drink called kykeon, made from water, barley and pennyroyal. She accepted the role of nursemaid to Demophon and the child prospered to the amazement of all who saw him. One night, Metaneira hid herself to see what Demeter was doing to make the child so strong and fair. She beheld

Demeter tucking the child up snuggly under a firebrand in the fire. Desperate with grief and worry she burst into the room and grabbed the child from the fire demanding that Demeter explain herself. Demeter was filled with rage, complaining loudly of the stupidity of humans. She said that she had intended to burn the mortality out of the child and make him like one of the gods, but now she could not. She revealed herself as the great Goddess Demeter and demanded that a temple be built in Eleusis in her honour, promising to teach her Mysteries to the people of the town who would observe them faithfully in perpetuity.

Demeter took up residence in her new temple, refusing to obey Zeus who sent several ambassadors first demanding and then pleading for her presence in Olympus. Zeus was becoming desperate, for while she was away from Olympus her face was veiled from the earth. The crops did not grow, there was no harvest and so the gods did not receive the rich offerings they were accustomed to. Finally, Demeter sent a message to Zeus, repeating her vow not to return to Olympus until she was reunited with Kore. Defeated, Zeus sent a message to Hades requesting that he allow Kore to leave his realm to meet her mother. Hades graciously acquiesced to the request but before the delighted girl left, he tricked her into eating four pomegranate seeds. Because of this, she was forced to return to Hades for four months of the year, during which the earth became barren and cold. For the rest of the year, while she was united with her mother in Olympus, the earth was warm and bright and fruitful. Meanwhile, the people of Eleusis joyfully maintained Demeter's temple and celebrated her Mysteries, as she had taught them, ever after.

It is worth recounting the tale in full, as it seems likely that many elements of it were dramatised in the process of initiation. The sitting, veiled, on a seat covered with a white fleece seems to have been re-enacted, and the drinking of kykeon was certainly central to the Mysteries. A key feature was also the torch bearing procession from Athens to Eleusis, presumably in imitation of Demeter's wandering around the earth in search of Kore. The cult was based on an allegorical understanding of the myth, assuming a wide and general familiarity with the story of Demeter and her daughter, but asserting that the true and hidden meaning of each of its elements was available only to initiates.

The origins of the cult centre in Eleusis are lost in the mists of history, but there is good evidence that the site was associated with the worship of a fertility goddess in the Bronze Age, certainly in the Mycenaean period (1550-1100 BCE) and possibly even back into the Minoan period as early as 3,000BCE. In the hymn, Demeter claims to have come originally from Crete, the home of the Minoan civilisation. The historian Herodotus (484-425 BCE) believed that many of the religious figures and practices of Greece originated in Crete, which was associated with arcane knowledge in the popular imagination. There may well be some truth in this. Minoan-style offering vessels have been found on the site and the idea of an afterlife connected with the cycles of nature more closely match those of the Minoan and Mycenaean cultures than those of Classical Greece, where only the elite can look forward to a glorious afterlife, while most can only expect the shadows of Hades. The name 'Eleusis' is Bronze Age in origin and the term 'Mysteries' is Mycenaean. There is archaeological evidence on the site from the Bronze Age of sacrifice, ritual bathing or libations and terracotta 'goddess figurines' that may, or may not, be identified with Demeter. It should be noted, however, that there is a four hundred year 'dark age' separating the Mycenaean and Classical periods. During this time, there seems to be a drastic reduction in literacy and it is not possible to be certain of any continuity of belief and worship in Eleusis during this time. Some have suggested an identification between Demeter and a widespread Ancient Near Eastern Neolithic Mother Goddess. There is no literary and little archaeological evidence to support this, but there are numerous cultural and material connections between Greece and Anatolia, so this interpretation is by no means impossible.

The Homeric Hymn to Demeter was written at a time when the cult was operated purely from Eleusis, with two families fulfilling the various roles in the priesthood on a hereditary basis. By the Sixth Century, however, Eleusis had come under the control of Athens and the processions by torchlight led from Athens to Eleusis, bringing significance and wealth to both. There was an official level to the Mysteries. Each year, Athens appointed a child to undergo initiation on behalf of the city to ensure prosperity and divine blessing. Many Emperors and philosophers underwent initiation meaning that the Mysteries became something of an open secret.

We know that the Mysteries were open to anyone who spoke Greek, regardless of age, gender or social standing, and as such they were significant in uniting society. The only criterion, other than being a Greek speaker, and therefore civilised, was to be of sound morals. Celsus, a Christian writing at the end of the Second Century CE, gives us the call to initiation proclaimed in Eleusis each year. "Come forward, whoever has a pure heart and a wise tongue; or else whoever is free of sin and whose soul is pure- You who are righteous and good- come forward." When Nero visited Greece, it was noticed that he avoided Eleusis and did not ask for initiation. The assumption was that he wished to avoid the embarrassment of being refused on the grounds of his many and various sins.

There were two levels of initiation. Only those who had undergone the first level (Myesis) were eligible, a year later, for the full initiation into the Mysteries (Epopteia).

The Lesser Mysteries were held in February and were a time for purification and preparation. The initiate knelt, veiled so that she could not see, and wrapped in a ram's skin. A winnowing fan, with clear agricultural implications was waved above her head and she held both an unlit torch and a snake, associated with both Demeter and Kore.

The Greater Mysteries were held in late summer, beginning on the 13th of Boedromion. This was the month in the local Attic calendar roughly corresponding to September and October, the time of the first harvests. On this date, the Athenian youths carried 'the holy things', the nature of which is uncertain, but which may have included the chest and basket mentioned below, from Eleusis to a special temple in Athens called the Eleusinion. They remained here until the 19th. During this time heralds called in the streets inviting those who were not *barbaroi* (non-Greek speakers) or criminals to take part in the Mysteries. Those who wished to undergo initiation bathed in the sea carrying a piglet that was subsequently sacrificed. Pigs are often associated with deities of the underworld. On the 19th, a huge procession, accompanied by the singing of special hymns and wild dancing as well as lighted torches reminiscent of the myth of Demeter carried the sacred objects back to Eleusis. The procession itself was a major part of the celebrations and had its own patron deity, Iacchos. The procession concluded at the Telesterion, or hall of initiation in Eleusis, having rested overnight at the Kallichorn Well, where Demeter had rested in her wandering and had met the daughters of Kelios. About half way to Eleusis, the procession crossed a bridge on which masked revellers shouted ritualised jokes and abuse at the initiates. Whether this was seen as a trial to test their resolve or was meant to make them laugh in imitation of Iambe coaxing a smile from Demeter is not clear. Perhaps it was both! On arriving in Eleusis, the celebrants broke their fast by drinking the kykeon, the same mixture of water, barley and pennyroyal as Demeter had broken her period of fasting with. There was a day of rest following the procession's arrival (which may have been much needed!) followed by a day devoted to rituals for the dead. Following this, on the ninth day of the festival, corresponding with the nine days of Demeter's wanderings, a bull was sacrificed and the procession started back for Athens.

All of this formed the public part of the festival, which is well documented in contemporary accounts. What is far less certain is what happened to those who underwent initiation during the festival. The initiation ritual was secret and so does not appear in any contemporary source in its entirety. It was, however, a fairly open secret as initiation was common and, indeed, virtually universal among the wealthy and educated classes. There are some 'in jokes' and oblique references in drama and literature from the time that an educated audience would have understood. There are also accounts from Christian writers who may well have been initiates themselves, but it should also be remembered that their chief purpose in writing was to discredit the cult. According to one such, Clement of Alexandria, the initiatory formula was:

I have fasted;
I have drunk the kykeon;
I have taken from the chest;
Having done the work, I have placed in the basket,
And from the basket into the chest.

Clement believes these symbolic actions to be sexual in nature, stating that the sacred objects in the chest include cakes, poppies, grain, pomegranates, a serpent and a model of female genitalia. It should also be noted, however, that many of these items also have clear agricultural symbolism as well as links to the story of Demeter and Kore which may have been dramatised in parts during the initiation rites. In Clement's defence, however, many sources do hint at a *hieros gamos* or sacred wedding as the climax of the rites. This, presumably, was between the Sky Father (Zeus) and the Earth or Grain Mother (Demeter or Kore). According to Hippolytus, the climax of the rite is the cry *'Hye Kye'* ('Rain,

Conceive') He also tells us that the hierophant, illuminated in the darkness of the initiation hall, cried out 'A holy child is born unto Brimo.' 'Brimo', meaning 'the strong one' may refer to Demeter, in which case the 'child' may be Kore, alternatively, 'Brimo' may refer to Kore, in which case the 'child' is less clear, but may be Dionysus. At some point initiates also beheld, in silence, a single harvested head of grain (a third candidate for the 'child'). Initiates were referred to as *Epoptai,* meaning 'the beholders' or 'those who have seen'.

It is certain that the initiation involved the drinking of kykeon. Since an ingredient of this is barley, and since barley famously has a psychotropic mould called ergot, there has been much speculation as to whether the initiation included a drug induced trance and possibly hallucinatory experiences. This is not impossible and it is certain that many initiates regarded their experience as spiritually transformatory and life changing. However, if too much ergotamine is consumed the result is very unpleasant indeed, resulting in convulsions and death. Given the huge numbers who underwent initiation each year it seems likely that we would have some record of at least a few fatalities and this is not the case. It is also true that another ingredient of the kykeon, pennyroyal, has hallucinogenic properties, and it is also toxic in large quantities, so there may well have been a degree of intoxication and altered consciousness involved. Whatever the properties of the drink, it seems likely to me that it was its symbolic value that was of central concern. The purpose of the drink may have been to take into one's physical body the earthly manifestation of the grain goddess in her forms as both Mother and Maiden.

We do know that that undergoing the Mysteries was believed to ensure a favourable afterlife for the initiate, and that the initiation itself was seen as a pre-figuring of death. Proclus, writing within living memory of the Mysteries, tells us, "On approaching death, the soul undergoes such an experience as those do who are initiated into the Great Mysteries. Thus, death and initiation closely correspond, word to word, and thing to thing. At first there are wanderings and labourious circuits and journeys through the dark, full of misgivings, where there is no consummation. Then, before the very end, come terrors of every kind, shivers and trembling and sweat and amazement. After this, a wonderful light meets the wanderer. He is admitted into pure meadow lands where are voices and dances and the majesty of holy sounds and sacred visions. Here, the new initiate, all rites completed, is at large." This blessed afterlife was not, however, purely through the favour of the gods. In Greek thought, humans were, of their very nature, mortal, while the gods were immortal. Between them was a divide that could not be crossed; the best a human could aspire to was a shadowy afterlife in the realm of Hades. The Mysteries offered a better hope not by making humans mortal, but by allowing them an apotheosis. That is they actually become united with the god (or in this case Goddess) who is already immortal and in this way they transcend mortality. The consumption of kykeon may have been a vital part of this process. Thus, the initiate becomes both Kore, buried in the earth as the planted grain and the maiden kidnapped by death; and Demeter, the mature grain that has transcended this apparent death. The grain, the Mother, the Maiden and the initiate are One, and so the initiate has already become an immortal. Death has no more relevance. If this is the case it is clear why early Christian writers were so keen to discredit the Mysteries!

Eleusis was a cult centre with some sort of association with an agricultural goddess from the Bronze Age until, along with the Oracle at Delphi and other great sites of Classical Paganism, it was closed down on the orders of the Christian emperor, Theodosius in 393CE. Its importance to the ancient world is summed up by Cicero, writing in the Second Century BCE who says of the Eleusinian Mysteries, "From them we have learned the rudiments (*initia*) as they are called, which are, in fact, the fundamental principles of living and thereby have received a rule, not only of happy living, but of dying with a better hope."

Unlike Delphi, Eleusis has almost completely disappeared from the modern popular imagination. The ruins are preserved as a tourist site, but they are not widely visited. When I was there in 2008 it took a while to convince the travel guide that I really did want to go there, and he was even more surprised that I stayed more than a few minutes. The site has a fence around it with a single ticket booth. Nothing else of interest is in the area. There were only one or two other visitors while I was there. The remains of the Hall of Initiation give some impression of the size of the Mysteries that were celebrated there. The processional way that leads to it is lined with the remains of statues set up by various emperors, officials and dignitaries from around the Roman world as evidence of their piety, and their wealth. It seems a sad fate for a site that was once at the very centre of Greek, and later Roman cultural, spiritual and religious life. For me, the most powerful experience of the site is to be found about half way along the surviving part of the processional way where it passes a natural cave in the rock next to which stands a tiny shrine to Hades, one of the oldest buildings on the site. It is quite possible that on this spot some sort of ritual was enacted that showed the triumphant return of Kore from the kingdom of Hades to the world of the living and her Mother's embrace. This, then, may be the original site of the gateway to the underworld.

Delphic Oracles ~ Irisanya Moon

"O Phoebus, from your throne of truth,
From your dwelling-place at the heart of the world,
You speak to men.
By Zeus' decree no lie comes from there,
No shadow to darken the word of truth.
Zeus sealed by an everlasting right
Apollo's honour, that all may trust
With unshaken faith when he speaks.
Mythology by Edith Hamilton

Situated high on the southern slope of Mount Parnassus is Delphi. Sometimes known as the *omphalos*, or the navel, of the world, Delphi was considered by some to be the most important shrine in Greece. This temple of Apollo was sought out by gods and travelers who wanted guidance and answers to their most pressing questions. And in the world where males seemed to dominate much of Greek culture, the voice of wisdom and divination was that of a woman oracle – the Pythia.

Etymologically the word Oracle, from the Latin *oraculum* from *orare* 'to speak' and 'to pray', suggests the need for a way to communicate with the divine was of great importance during the time of the Greek gods. Not only was this seen in the temple that Apollo had at Delphi, but also in the many other smaller shrines and temples that were placed in cities. There would be shrines to particular deities where you might perform (or have performed) various acts of divination, e.g. casting of lots.

One of the more common methods of oracular work was dream incubation, in which a person might sleep in the temple to a particular god and ask for the answer to their query in a dream. Another form of oracular work might look like someone inspired by a god and then answering the question of a person directly while in that trance-like state.

The priestess who was the oracle was first a young virgin girl, but after one of the oracles was kidnapped and violated, women over the age of fifty were chosen for the role – though still dressed as young girls. There is mystery surrounding how a Pythia was chosen for the role, but as one would die and need to be replaced, the priestesses of the area were likely to discuss potential candidates and vote for the one who was deemed most appropriate for the role. Early times called for more educated Pythiai, while later times were less focused on schooling.

It is thought there were three Pythiai available at all times, so two could be available for prophesies on the certain day of the month, while one would be resting. Though the life of a Pythia was one of great importance, it was also tiring and often resulted in the women having shorter lifespans.

In addition to the Pythiai there were lifetime priests of Apollo, chosen from the citizens of Delphi, as well as hosioi who helped in the operations of the temple.

Delphi would be open to visitors once a month on the seventh day of the Delphic month (Apollo's birthday), and not during the three winter months. Travelers would ask questions about the mundane, war, politics, and religion, as well as love and health. But the answers were not always as straightforward as the questioner might hope and many times the traveler might leave with more questions.

If a consultant (traveler) was committed to going to Delphi, they were willing to travel across the Gulf of Corinth or across the vast mountains. It was a trip that would take a long time and it was often a trip that was only made once.

A person who wanted to go to the Delphic oracle would need to have a sponsor, and they would need to bring a ritual cake (or pie, pelanos) and an animal to sacrifice before the prophecy could occur. The person (sometimes known as a supplicant) would also need to prepare themselves for the visit with the oracle. This might include conversations about how to phrase their question, presenting gifts, all before visiting with the oracle.

The Pythiai were considered those who spoke for the gods and spoke the words of the gods. These women could hear the petitions and questions of the visitors and pass on answers in return. These women were not only tasked to facilitate communication, but also to deliver important messages to aid in the movement of the military across the lands.

When it was time for the Pythia to move into her oracular role, she would bathe in the Castalian spring and then drink from a sacred spring in Cassotis. Her head would be covered in a purple veil throughout, allowing her to attain deeper insight and trance.

The purification rites would continue with holy water sprinkled throughout the temple. Laurel branches were offered to Apollo, as well as money, and a sacrificial goat.

The Pythia would remove her purple veil and put on a plain white dress. The goat would be sacrificed and if the animal did not tremble from the hooves up, the visitor would not be able to ask their question as that was a sign of rejection by the gods.

After these preparations, she would enter the temple and take her place on a sacred golden tripod where she would chew on laurel leaves (according to some texts). In doing so, she would begin to enter an altered state and then begin to answer the questions of the visitor.

Since Gaia was considered to be the original goddess of the temple (and some say that Apollo stole Delphi from her), the priestesses of Delphi would start every ritual with an invocation to Her:

I give first place of honour in my prayer to her
who of the gods first prophesied the Earth.
Aeschylus, *Eumenides*

The visitor could only ask questions and was not permitted to write down the answers. Scribes fulfilled that role in addition to interpreting the messages. While many of the messages were unclear or unintelligible, they were still recorded in verse.

Sometimes answers came as 'Yes' or 'No' via the throwing of beans. Many of the answers would be delivered in a poetic manner, offering images and metaphors for the visitors.

Many texts describe two distinct trance states that the Pythiai experienced. One was an altered state of semi-consciousness in which the priestess remained on the tripod and answered questions with a different or strange voice. Another state was likened to a frenzied running around while crying out in gibberish. (These states often preceded the Pythia's death and the need to replace her by a new priestess).

[T]he seat of the oracle is a cavern hollowed down in the depths ... from which arises pneuma [breath, vapor, gas] that inspires a divine state of possession. Strabo (c. 64 BCE-CE 25)

Some might say this is because the answers of the gods are hard to understand, while others believe the Pythiai were under the influence of hallucinogens. According to geological research, there is some concern that the temple was situated on a natural source of hydrocarbon gases.

The Pythiai are sometimes shown under the influence of the vapours, and this research might support this hypothesis. But while some might dismiss the power of the prophesy due to its drug-related inspiration, there are others that hold the nearly 600 questions and answers to be directly from the gods. Having been written down per oral tradition, one might never be able to know for certain. And perhaps that's the true power of an oracle.

Others say that oleander was the cause of the Pythia's visions, as it can cause the same symptoms as being in a trance or altered state. The leaves can also be burned and the smoke can have a hallucinogenic effect.

Some scholars have pointed out that many prophesies were influenced by gold offerings with the promise of more from the visitors if they didn't respond well to the Pythia's first answer. A prophesy could move from doom to hope, most notably in the prediction before the Battle of Salamis. While the initial prophesy showed a terrible loss, a subsequent divination revealed that a 'wooden wall' (interpreted as boats) would save the Greeks. And even in their outnumbered state, the Athenians did end up winning the naval battle.

But once the prophesy was given to the visitor, the work began for them. Not only did those who sought counsel need to travel and prepare before seeing the oracle, but they also needed to act upon the information they were given.

Whether the Delphic Oracles were under the power of plants or vapors or whether they were the direct line of communication to the gods, there are clear implications for the modern world in the steps a consultant would need to take in order to consult with the oracle.

- Travel – Choosing to embark on a long journey, in any time, is risky. You must be clear about the dangers you might face, the way others might perceive you, and the best course of travel. The ones who visited Delphi needed to be clear about the need for guidance from the Pythia. They would be tested along the way and only the commitment to asking the right question could be the motivation to continue the travels over mountains or sea. This travel also hindered many potential consultants of the oracle, as not everyone could afford to be away for such a long time or had the means to make a journey safely. Since the oracle was only available on one day a month (and only nine months out of the year), the journey needed to be timed correctly or else one might need to wait for another month before getting to ask a question. But there are initiatory implications with the journey from where you were to where you want to go. Once you leave, you will not return the same person, even if you don't see the oracle, and especially when you do see the oracle.

- Preparation – Even if the consultant made the journey to Delphi and arrived healthy, they still needed to work with attendants of the temple to prepare to meet the oracle. These preparations might take days to complete, with discussions about how to ask a question, purification rites, and activities to induce a trance-like state. The consultant needs to go into the temple as connected to the gods as possible and as ready to hear the answer they seek. The preparations and meeting the oracle might take an entire day, and this is after many weeks of travel to arrive on the right day. And these preparations also denote a commitment to follow through, to acting on the word of the gods.

- Asking the question – While asking the question seems to be the most important focus, it could be argued that listening to the answer is much more important. Not only is the answer something that was divined by the Pythia, but it was also something that would be translated by the person who heard the answer. With their own lens, and probably their own agenda, the consultant would hear what they wanted to hear … or they might hear what they needed to hear. Sitting and asking the question means there is no turning back, no turning off the knowledge that was presented. The consultant would know the words and would have to know them for the rest of their lives.

- Taking action – In acting on the advice of the gods, one's life can't help but change. The consultants and their sponsors would know the words of the gods and know what was suggested of them. The follow-through became the sacred charge to action and to never going back to the way things were before the knowledge was bestowed. Ignoring the gods is impossible.

At the entrance to the temple, Know Thyself, Nothing in Excess, and Make a Pledge and Mischief is Nigh, were carved into the stone, reminding all visitors of sacred advice from sages.

Knowing thyself (attributed to Thales of Miletus) means knowing what one needs and what one does not need. In going to the temple for guidance, the consultant needs to know what is in their best interest to ask ... and what they might want to find out on their own. Only in knowing what is truly important and what is truly valuable can one enter the temple.

One can also look at Know Thyself as a reminder that if one asks the gods for guidance, they must also listen to the gods and their answers. Not all answers will be the ones that were expected and not all details will be the ones that come with simple actions to take.

To follow the idea of Nothing in Excess (attributed to Solon of Athens or Cleobulus of Lindos), there must be discipline and focus. One must know what is too much for them (know thyself) and then labor to avoid such things. It is also the reminder that anything that seems to be good is not necessarily something that one should continue. There is balance in the universe, and that balance comes from limiting greed and other temptations of excess.

And Make a Pledge and Mischief is Nigh (attributed to Thales of Miletus) is the inscription that seems to remind the consultant that things happen when you make a pledge to the gods. Whether meeting the oracle or not, any promise to the gods means the gods are a part of the process too. They might have other ways of moving something forward and of making something happen that might look like mischief ... and even mayhem.

We can't move away from the fact that the Delphic Oracles are just as relevant today as they were in Classical times. In their era, they presented opportunity for women to control the fates of men by becoming conduits for the gods' messages. And today, their stories and their abilities remind us that prophesy is just as dangerous as it is instructive.

No matter the source of wisdom, the Pythiai speak in languages that relay information and possibility, poetry and challenge. Do we dare to follow the words of the gods? Do we dare not to?

Christian
Goddess

The Virgin Mary ~ Laurie Martin-Gardner

Today, her names are many: Blessed Mother, Our Lady, Mother Most Pure, Our Lady of Grace. Elaborate and beautiful names sing her praises and fill the fervent prayers of the faithful. But as a humble young woman in the city of Nazareth, she was known simply as Mary. Her story begins with a message, delivered by the archangel Gabriel. She is to birth a king, a savior of mankind, the promise of prophecies long told among her people. And while within her own heart, she ponders the significance of all the angel reveals to her, she answers Gabriel's proclamation with simple eloquence: "Behold the handmaiden of the Lord; be it unto me according to thy word" (Luke 1:38).

Mary's words, and submission to the will of God, set into motion a religious movement that would forever alter the path of humanity. The story of Christianity, in a sense, begins with her. And yet, we know very little about the woman that would become the Mother of the Lord. Who was the true Mary of Nazareth?

The Gospel of Luke provides the most Biblical insight into the Blessed Mother. We know from the account recorded in the Gospel that Mary is a virgin, betrothed to a man named Joseph. As a first-century Jewish woman, we can assume that she was quite young at the time of her betrothal. The Gospel does not record her actual age, but it was common for a girl of the time to be wed as young as 12.

Luke goes on to tell us that it was during the period of her betrothal (which typically lasted several months), that the angel of the Lord appeared to Mary and greeted her as "blessed art thou among women" (Luke 1:28). After soothing Mary's fears, Gabriel revealed God's plans to her:"And behold, thou shalt conceive in thy womb, and bring forth a son, and shalt call his name Jesus. He shall be great, and shall be called the Son of the Highest" (Luke 1:31-32). Mary did not question the words of the angel, but she did seek clarification. She was, after all, a virgin. She questioned the angel saying, "How shall this be, seeing I know not a man?" (Luke 1:34). Gabriel explained to the bewildered maiden that the spirit of the Lord would come to her and through it she would conceive the son of God. He then gave Mary a sign, telling her that her cousin Elisabeth had also conceived even in her old age. "For with God nothing shall be impossible," he promised Mary. And she consented to be the vessel of the Son of God.

Mary then left Nazareth and traveled to Judah to visit Elisabeth and her husband, Zechariah. The Gospel of Luke tells us that when Mary greeted Elisabeth, the child within Elisabeth's womb (a child who would become John the Baptist) leapt within her and the Holy Spirit filled her. She then greeted Mary, repeating the greeting of the angel Gabriel, "Blessed art thou among women, and blessed is the fruit of thy womb" (Luke 1:42). Upon hearing Elisabeth's words, Mary's heart was quieted and she knew that the angel had spoken the truth to her. She went on to praise God in what would become known as the Magnificant and stayed several months in the home of her cousin.

Upon arriving back in Nazareth, it was quite obvious that the young Mary was pregnant. This, of course, troubled Joseph greatly. Being pregnant out of wedlock was no trivial matter at the time. Joseph could have easily cast Mary away or even have had her killed for her indiscretion. Mary assured him that the child she carried was the son of God and that she had known no man. While Joseph took the time to ponder the proper course to take, the Gospel of Matthew states that Joseph was visited in a dream by an angel of the Lord. The angel told him, "fear not to take unto thee Mary thy wife, for that which is conceived in her is of the Holy Ghost" (Matthew 1:20). Upon waking, Joseph went to Mary and took her as his wife as the Lord had commanded.

While pregnant with Jesus, a decree issued by Caesar Augustus that "all the world should be taxed" (Luke 2:1), forced Joseph and Mary to make the journey from Nazareth to Bethlehem, the city of David. It was in Bethlehem that Mary felt the first pangs of labor. Finding no room for them at the inn, Mary gave birth and placed the infant Jesus in a manger. He was visited there by shepherds who had heard of his birth from an angel of the Lord and later by the magi who had followed the Star of Bethlehem to find the newborn king.

Although the story of the nativity is one that is familiar to most, the rest of Mary's life is told only in brief bits scattered throughout the Gospels. We know from the book of Matthew that Joseph is warned in a dream to flee with his family into the land of Egypt. King Herod, after hearing from the magi that a King of the Jews had been born in Bethlehem, ordered the slaughter of all the male infants near the city in a horrific event that would come to be known as the Massacre of the Innocents. By abiding the warning in his dream, the holy family escaped the persecution of Herod and did not return until after his death.

Mary appears sporadically throughout the remainder of the Gospels. We know from the gospels that she presented her son to the Temple forty days after his birth, as was customary. It was during this trip that Mary, through the holy Simeon, first learned of the tragedy that would befall her precious son. Then, in the only Biblical account of Jesus as a boy, Mary is shown as a worried mother searching for her missing son at the Temple. Later at a wedding in Cana, she appears again to request the assistance of Jesus, prompting the performance of his first miracle of turning water into wine. She then appears again, seeking out her son among his disciples. During the crucifixion, she stands at the foot of the cross as Jesus dies. Finally, in her last Biblical appearance, the book of Acts records simply that she was among the apostles upon their return from the Mount of Olives. After that, the Bible is silent on the fate of the Blessed Mother.

Although she speaks on only four occasions in the Bible,

the devoted and mournful Mary captured the hearts of early Christians. Marian veneration can be traced back as far as the second century but was likely based on even older traditions. Her blessed life inspired countless early church leaders and religious philosophers to attempt to piece together more of Mary's story. While not considered as authoritative as the books of the Bible, the traditions that emerged would become integral parts of Catholic and Eastern Orthodox beliefs.

The Gospel of James, an apocryphal text probably written around CE 145, is one vitally important text that attempted to fill in the missing details of the Virgin Mary's story. It is stated in the text that Mary is the child of Saint Joachim and Saint Anne. Much like in the story of Elisabeth and Zechariah, Anne and Joachim were advanced in age before God rewarded their devotion with the birth of a daughter. In this account, an angel was sent to Anne to announce the conception of a child that "shall be spoken of in all the world". This, and other similar recounts of the Holy Mother's conception and birth, would come to be known as the Immaculate Conception. To the early Christian fathers, it was obvious that Mary had been blessed by God before she was even conceived. In this way, Mary was free from the curse of original sin and was born and lived in complete perfection. St. Augustine, an early Christian theologian and philosopher, affirmed this belief by saying "through her birth, the nature inherited from our first parents (Adam and Eve) is changed".

When she was only three years old, the text continues, Anne and Joachim presented Mary to the Temple of Jerusalem where she lived and studied as a consecrated virgin. When she neared the age of marriage, the temple priest decided that she should be given as a bride to a man that God would choose with a certain sign. Although much older than Mary and with children from a previous marriage, Joseph was chosen by God to be the Blessed Mother's husband.

It is also in the Gospel of James that the idea of Mary's perpetual virginity is first recorded. According to this belief, Mary was not only a virgin at the time of Jesus' birth but, as a consecrated virgin, remained one for the entirety of her life. And although she entered into marriage with Joseph, the relationship was chaste and pure. For early church fathers, it seemed inconceivable that a normal human child should ever occupy the same womb as the son of God. Mary's perpetual virginity and perfect sanctity were seen as necessary to ensure that she would be worthy of bearing the savior, Jesus Christ. Therefore, Mary was not chosen as the Mother of God because of any unique personal trait but because she had been blessed by Almighty God.

Another common interest in the early church was the manner in which the Virgin Mary died. Although the Bible is silent on her death, the Gospel of James and other apocryphal texts claim that she was blessed not only in life but also in death. Some accounts record that she died a normal human death and was then taken into Heaven after three days. This belief, or the miracle of Dormition, is an important facet of the Orthodox tradition. The Catholic Church, however, embraced texts that stated that Mary did not die a natural death. Instead, she was taken from earth, both body and soul, into Heaven. For Catholics, this belief became known as the Assumption and is accepted as an infallible doctrine.

Although universally revered within the realm of Christianity, there are distinct differences in Marian reverence between Catholics, Orthodox Christians, and Protestants. These differences arise, primarily, through each group's interpretation of the Biblical accounts and extraneous materials. While Protestants largely accept only that Mary was the mother of Jesus, the Catholic and Orthodox churches hold her in a central role within the faith.

Mary is an essential figure among the world's 1.2 billion Catholics. Her praises are heard in countless prayers and hymns, and a multitude of holy days celebrate her life as the

Mother of the Church. All Catholics accept four Marian beliefs; her own Immaculate Conception, her perpetual virginity, her Assumption into heaven, and her role as the Mother of God. Members of the Catholic Church also view Mary as a powerful *mediatrix*. Prayers are offered to Mary with the belief that she will take a person's prayers to her Holy Son on the behalf of the believer. Some Christians outside of the Catholic Church see this as bordering on blasphemy and believe that Catholics are actually worshiping Mary. The Church, however, insists that Mary is only venerated and not worshiped as a divine being. Requesting her to intercede, many Catholics say, is no different than a Protestant asking a trusted friend to say a prayer on his or her behalf.

Orthodox Christians also do not worship Mary, instead holding her in a place of high honor. It is most often within the Eastern Orthodox Church that we hear Mary referred to as *Theotokos*, Mother of God. This title was first decreed in CE 431 at the Council of Ephesus, a meeting of bishops attempting to reach a consensus on church doctrine. The Orthodox Church rejects the idea of Mary's immaculate conception but embraces the idea of her perpetual virginity and absence of sin. Hymns to Mary, the Theotokia, are extremely important in the Orthodox tradition and place Mary as the highest among the saints. Feasts and holy days are devoted to Mary as they are in Catholicism.

In general, Protestants reject all or most of the Marian dogma held by the Catholic and Orthodox Churches. Most Protestants agree that Mary should be held in reverence as the chosen mortal mother of the Son of God, but that she is afforded no other special significance. They reject all concepts of her sinless nature, her immaculate conception, and her supernatural death or resurrection. They affirm that their beliefs are based purely on the text of the New Testament as opposed to the inclusion of non-canonical texts by the Catholic and Orthodox churches. In recent years, however, some Protestants have begun to reevaluate the Holy Mother, finding new ways to honor her within the confines of the Protestant belief system.

Beyond the scope of the Christian Church, we can also find Mary in the Islamic holy book, the Qur'an. Here she is given an honored position as the greatest of all women. The Blessed Virgin is the only woman to be named within the Qur'an and is even given her own Sura, or chapter, within the book. Perhaps just as surprisingly, Mary has also been embraced by New Age spiritualists and modern pagans. Often equated with other great Mother Goddesses, the appeal of the Virgin Mary is not limited to the confines of religion.

While church officials may argue over the details of Marian dogma, believers have little doubt in the power of the Holy Mother. For centuries, the faithful have ascribed to the Virgin Mary a multitude of wondrous and healing miracles. Often appearing to young children living in terrible crisis, thousands of sightings of the Virgin are reported every year. Often she brings messages of hope and love or powerful glimpses into the future. On some occasions, physical signs or miracles also accompany her appearance. One of the most famous of these reputed signs was the "spinning sun" seen over Medjugorje after repeated visits of the Holy Mother to six Herzegovinian children. Another is the sacred waters of Lourdes, discovered as a small spring by a young girl who reported she was led to its location by the Virgin Mary. Hundreds of physical and spiritual healings have been attributed to these locations and others like them around the world. Each miraculous encounter with the Holy Mother is investigated by the Catholic Church in a long and detailed procedure. And while most of these miracles are dismissed by the Church, it does little to discourage the faithful who believe in the unwavering love and power of the Virgin Mary.

Regardless of the limits placed on her by religious tradition, the importance of the Virgin Mary cannot be overemphasized. Her image is one of the most reproduced and recognizable in the world. Her story as the devoted and mournful mother transcends religion, making her a more accessible figure than Christ often appears. Her name is whispered in worried prayers and reverberated through great halls. Those who claim to have miraculously encountered the Virgin describe her as exuding pure and undying love for all people. Indeed, if we are to believe that God is the Father of all mankind, certainly that makes Mary, the Mother of God, the mother of us all. When once asked about the Virgin Mary, Pope Francis answered simply, "She is my mamá."

Perhaps, therein lies the imperishable nature of Mary. No religious context is needed to understand the love of a mother. It is human nature to seek out the open arms of one whose love is gentle and unwavering. Mary transcends religion. She is not bound to Christianity and her love is not bound only to the worthy. Just as she encouraged Jesus to perform his first miracle in Cana, she encourages those that seek her out to have faith and to extend love to all people. A common theme among her visitations to her faithful is her deep concern for the state of humanity. She is the worried mother, hoping to save her children from great hardships through her guidance. Mary is the epitome of motherly love and unwavering devotion to God. She is a both a beacon of hope and an ideal to strive toward. Her presence is felt in vaulted cathedrals, crumbling shacks, empty fields, and anywhere a heart calls out in need. Pope Pius IX summarized her role beautifully·and simply writing, "For God has committed to Mary the treasury of all good things, in order that everyone may know that through her are obtained every hope, every grace, and all salvation."

Mary Magdalene ~ Dorothy Abrams

How is a human woman in history also a Goddess? Isn't deity an Us/Them inequality? Aren't there lines humans cannot cross? Is it ego, pride and greed to think otherwise? No, no and no. Humans can transcend the boundaries into the Godhead as demonstrated in all the spiritual story books available to us. The dual nature available to all people of faith is an ill kept secret. Any of us might become a Goddess and a Human. That is what the awakening Mary Magdalene found and the church has denied. A closer look will show she is Goddess.

To begin with, the historical woman Mary Magdalene is identified in the New Testament as a disciple of Jesus, one with resources and wealth, likely the hostess in the upper room of her home where the last supper was held. She is a friend of the family. She is the woman from whom Jesus cast seven demons. She is the disciple he kissed on the lips. According to her own *Gospel of the Beloved,* she was given advanced teachings which the male disciples resented in a display of sexist indignation. She was first at the tomb, first to see the risen Jesus, first to motivate the disciples to get on with it and spread the Gospel without fear of government and synagogue opposition. That is the written New Testament record.

Speculation opens up a tradition in which she was married to Jesus at the wedding in Cana. He performed his first miracle there, turning water into wine as if the party was his responsibility. Some suggest their blood line is the royal blood of Europe. Others suggest she is the Holy Grail, that the chalice is a symbol of her womb. Mythology takes over and gives us fascinating possibilities in *Holy Blood Holy Grail* and the Dan Brown page turner *The DaVinci Code.* Was that Mary at the last supper leaning on Jesus' chest? Or was it a male disciple, John perhaps? Which is more scandalous?

The church fathers evidently wanted to skirt her potential as a spiritual equal of the disciples if not Jesus himself. For hundreds of years she was confused with the adulteress Jesus converted in John 7. Thanks to Pope Gregory I in the 7th century that woman plus Mary of Bethany and the anonymous woman in Luke 7 are all identified as Mary Magdalene. There is no evidence in the Bible or elsewhere for any of that, but it leaves the Magdalene with a shady reputation. For the church fathers she was a lesson in the questionable character of women in general. Any enlightenment she carried was besmirched by her gender as well as her past. Despite this, the 21st-century Pope Francis I elevated her memorial day of July 22 to a Feast Day putting her on a footing nearly equal to the Apostles. She still is referenced as a converted prostitute by some but she is also Apostle to the Apostles, an example of God's mercy in the year of Jubilee 2016 and a saint of power within the church. That's not quite the same as clearing her reputation. Instead it is a way of giving the male God all the credit for the poor sinner woman's success. None of that, of course, makes her a Goddess.

And what about those demons? If she was possessed does that mean she was controlled by evil? How does she then become a Goddess? The likely explanation for that is in "casting out demons" Jesus cured Mary of clinical depression. The medieval monks called it acedia, the noonday demon. It is the despair that we are nothing, incompetent, foolish times seven. We believe that our work is sand, our words ashes. Acedia appears in the face of the bright noonday sun and turns any joy we might find into self-pity and inaction. For Mary to become what she was capable of being, she had to be healed from seven of those deep demons of self-doubt. How did he cast them out? Worthlessness is with love and validation. I find her restoration indicative of their marriage, their erotic passion and sexual healing. She learned of her own worth because it was reflected in his eyes. That is what real love does for us. Instead of the Us/Them inequality we see the result of synergy. 1 + 1 > 2.

Early church history provides other scraps of information. Modestus, Patriach of Jerusalem in the 7th century wrote that after the crucifixion Mary Magdalene lived in Ephesus with John Mark and Mary the mother of Jesus until her martyrdom. Christians suggest the Magdalene is buried on Mt. Pion in Ephesus Turkey with other early church leaders like Timothy. More intricate theories say she escaped to Marseille, France, with her daughter Sarah and with or without Jesus depending on whether one thinks he survived the crucifixion or was resurrected but not ascended.

We should note The Temple of Artemis is also in Ephesus. There are parallels between the Goddess and the disciple. Both have close allegiances with the Sun God. Artemis is sister to Apollo and Magdalene is the confidante of Jesus who himself is an Apollo figure, sun god and all. The women are queens of heaven. They nurture humanity. Artemis is chaste. She is independent and walks her path alone. The Magdalene is a woman of independent means, perhaps a chaste Essene or perhaps the wife of Jesus. She follows her own conscience. Artemis is the Goddess of the Hunt. The Magdalene is an Apostle of evangelism, so like a hunt for souls and conversion.

The sister Temple of Artemis was in Marseille where the Magdalene may have fled her persecutors so the parallels between the Magdalene and the Goddess of the Hunt continue. Many have her buried in a cave in France. Dan Brown took it a step further and placed her body in Rosslyn Chapel in Scotland though everyone there says the idea is ridiculous. They insist there are good reasons not to open the rooms beneath the chapel; such privacy has no connection to the Holy Grail. And no, you can't take pictures.

Another fascinating suggestion is that the holy family moved to Glastonbury for a time, where Sarah stayed and worked. Then Mary returned to France. Or maybe not. Maybe they stayed in Glastonbury. I particularly like that theory from personal experience. Let me tell you a story.

In 2007 my husband Merlin and I visited Glastonbury Abbey with a local guide who knows the esoteric connections and ley lines better than most. She pointed out on the side of a building in the complex the names of Mary and Jesus carved into the exterior wall, seemingly apropos to nothing. Then she pointed to the two gravesites commonly identified in legend as the graves of Arthur and Guinevere. The sites are just a few yards off to the side. I stood there taking in the energy and felt it hum, but I couldn't tell who was the source of that vibrational wave. Something was there, but what?

Later in the St. John the Baptist Church, a saint associated with the Magdalene, the tour guide pointed out the black stone grave covers on either side of the altar. One had an etched male figure, the other a female. Were these the covers from the graves in the abbey grounds? Or were they some unidentified merchant and wife? I stepped into the space between them and was nearly floored. The same humming was amplified in the church and told me the connection to the anonymous gravesites was real, though unexplained. I spent years in my past as a devotee of Jesus. I thought the vibration was more than familiar. I took a front pew seat back far enough to clear my head. I measured the field. The love and devotion between the couple escalated to a kundalini intensity. These are no ordinary merchants. I don't think they are the King and Queen of Camelot either. I suspect we have traces of Jesus and the Magdalen there in Glastonbury. Frankly I would still be sitting here in the midst of a trance in St. John's Church if my friends hadn't insisted I get up and leave. Part of me is still there.

The idea the sacred couple may be buried in Glastonbury is not as crazy as it sounds. Joseph of Arimathea was a metal merchant and wealthy relative of Jesus. He also seems to be a friend of the Magdalene. He and his thorn tree walking stick are identified as the founder of Glastonbury Abbey after the death and resurrection of Jesus. Prior to that, in the silent years before Jesus was 30 he could have traveled to the tin and lead mines along the west coast of England on business and perhaps to confer with the magicians in Glastonbury. Even if he did not visit in person, when it was time to disappear from the Mediterranean basin, his uncle could have moved the family out of harm's way in France into the wilds of the north where magic happened. People traveled in those days more than we think. First-century paganism was alive and well in the Isle and any monks living there had not yet drained the surrounding lands.

But if Jesus and the Magdalene were buried there, where are their remains? No one knows. Whether or not the graves held famous people or ordinary merchants, the bones were disturbed by monks digging at the direction of Henry II. They were later reinterred in the Lady Chapel at the Abbey in 1278 in front of King Edward I. The exhumation was not performed scientifically and the results reveal nothing worthwhile. Further, making the site connected to the famous legend of Arthur brought pilgrims and money for a medieval construction project. That calls any conclusions into question as a marketing plan. The destruction of the abbey by Henry VIII during the English Reformation in 1539 disturbed the burial again and the bones disappeared. The original grave was 3 times as deep as a conventional grave. The bodies were contained together in a large log. Halfway down the deep grave, a cross with Arthur's name was added, but it wasn't on the log. We are left with myth, legend and no evidence.

So even as apparent historical characters, Mary Magdalene and Jesus are shadowy figures of faith. You pick the version of their lives you like best and hang your soul on it. Or not. Believers know how Jesus the son of man combined his human and divine nature to also be God. Or they think they do. Just how an avatar walks the earth with one foot in both dimensions is a divine mystery to me. If one can accept he did it, then why not she? They both elevated thought, life, spirit into a sort of hybrid demigod existence in which they performed miracles, healing and leaps of consciousness for themselves and people around them. The multiple Gods of all pantheons have done that across the millennia. Why not the Magdalene? That's one way a human woman becomes a Goddess, by association, teaching and practice, also known as magic.

But there is more for us to learn. There is the challenge she and he lay at the feet of the rest of us. What they did we can do and more. The real essence of being a Christian Goddess, or God for that matter, is to transform the people who look at their lives and say *I can do that*. I can do that, not out of my ego but out of association. That is what the other disciples did. They learned they could heal people, perform miracles, and overcome their fears of stepping out from human limitations. They learned it from Jesus when he was with them. They learned it from Mary when she told them what else he said. They learned it from the infusion of wisdom through that other biblical Goddess Sophia commonly referred to as the Holy Spirit. If we doubt ourselves we also doubt Mary Magdalene, but what if we didn't?

The transformation of ordinary people into demigods, those who combine human and divine souls, who make things happen, who live magic is not limited to Christianity. In fact the mythology adopted by Christian institutions prevents that transformation from happening. The Church has darkened the vision instead of opening it to more light. They say the greater miracles are answered prayers, not raising the dead nor healing with a touch. However, western mysticism, witchcraft, and interaction with the old Gods and Goddesses who predate Jesus and the Magdalene create the divine transformation for those who dare. There are few who risk such a journey. Easily labeled delusional, crazy, heretical, mad we draw back from the advanced teachings the Magdalene held. We look away when the Goddess says "Thou art god". We don't do the reading or meditation that might open the door into that light. It's too frightening. Artemis would take us there. Isis, Hecate, Grandmother Spider. Any number of powerful figures wait patiently for us to wake up and realize we are only living the human half of our lives. The Magdalene is one such Goddess asking us to follow her example and rescue ourselves and the world. I wonder what we might do if we were not asleep?

The 21st century is a good time to wake up. We are needed as avatars to heal the earth. The ocean needs an infusion of oxygen. The plastic afloat in the seas needs collection. The pipeline ruptures need to be staunched and cleaned up. The politicians need a green earth vision. Petroleum based power grids need to be replaced with wind, solar and geothermal grids. Justice and compassion need to be extended to all people in all faiths. Violence and hate must recede in the face of love. World leaders must step out to accept people who are "the other". Everyone must stop lying and twisting events to gain power. If any of that is to happen, we who know how must perform magic. We must create transformation. Standing up when others shrink back, calling people to responsibility and showing faith is our mission, even as the light in human consciousness dims. Mary Magdalene can speak through us, and has been waiting a long time for Christians, Pagans, Jews, Muslims all to connect and create the new heaven and new earth.

Female Mystics ~ Shaun Johnson

From the mid to late Middle Ages, between the East-West Schism of 1054 and the Reformation of the Sixteenth Century, many of the most significant Christian Mystics were female, at a time when women had very little status within society. Their visionary experiences gave them a voice and an authority they otherwise wouldn't have had, though not all wholeheartedly welcomed the idea. Mary Magdalen del Pazzi (1566-1607), for example, came to the conclusion that interaction with God was subjective and deeply personal, and as such rejected the written word. If ever left alone with notes taken by others when she experienced visions in trance, she would burn them.

There was a specific process women needed to go through for their works to reach a wider audience, involving the sanction and approval of higher religious authorities, invariably men. Hildegard Von Bingen, for example, sought guidance from Bernard of Clairvaux, himself one of the most important Christian Mystics of the age, who interceded with the Pope on her behalf to authorise the continued transcribing of her visions. This wasn't just a bureaucratic process, as most female Christian Mystics were writing during the time of the Inquisitions, when many of their works could be classed as potentially heretical, particularly as they advocated a direct and personal interaction with God or the Divine, without the need for intermediaries, implicitly challenging the authority of the clergy. A failure to go through the accepted procedure could have serious consequences, as can be seen in the case of Marguerite Porete (c.1248/50-1310), whose visionary writings on the freedom of the soul led to her imprisonment, the condemnation of her works and her being burnt at the stake.

The first prominent female Christian Mystic was the multi-talented Hildegard von Bingen (1098-1174), a painter, poet, composer, physician and healer, who almost set the template for the female Mystics who were to follow, being of noble birth, precarious health and experiencing intense altered states of consciousness from an early age. Being the tenth child, she was, as was customary at that time, handed over to the church as a form of tithe, at aged eight being put into the care of Jutta von Spanheim, an anchoress who lived in an enclosed cell attached to the Benedictine cloister of Saint Disibod. Since Hildegard had been having strange experiences since the age of three, when she saw "a brightness so great [her] soul trembled," it's not inconceivable her family were happy to get rid of her. It was common for wealthy families to put girls and women who were unusual or rebellious, or had disabilities or emotional issues, into convents, paying a dowry as a means of literally marrying them off to God.

In 1141, aged 42, Hildegard experienced a vision of blinding light, during which she was told to "write what you see and hear". Over the course of the next ten years, she detailed 24 of her visions, with accompanying commentaries, published as 'Scivias', an extraordinary mix of intense explorations of various aspects of scripture, creation, prophesy, the apocalyptic and in particular the search for wisdom. For her, God was *lux vivens*, the living light, this reflected in her descriptions and paintings, with their striking use of light and color.

Clare of Assisi (1195-1253), a disciple and associate of Francis of Assisi, was a quiet and studious child from a very wealthy family whose life changed after she saw Francis preaching in 1210. Sometime later, when her family were about to have her married off, she escaped through a back door to join Francis and his followers, where Francis cut off her hair, gave her a hair shirt to wear and welcomed her as a follower of God. Her family tried unsuccessfully to get her back, and in the end both her sisters and her mother joined her. Clare embraced a life of poverty, giving up her possessions and handing over all her money to the poor. She lived an ascetic lifestyle, involving excessive fasting to the extreme that she was too weak to walk for many years, and performed mortifications so severe that Francis himself had to intervene. She was able to become so enwrapped in prayer and devotion that she could stay in a semi-conscious state for 24 hours at a time. She was the first woman to write a rule for monastics, but only a small number of letters and fragments remain of her writings.

Where much is known of Clare of Assisi's life, and little of her written work, for many female Mystics the opposite is true, with little known of the lives of Mechtchild of Magdeberg, Hadewijch of Brabant and Julian of Norwich, except that which is documented in their writings and through sparse details found in other records. Mechtchild of Magdeberg (c.1210-1282) was the first European Mystic known to have written in the vernacular, and lived in a Beguine community for 40 years, before fleeing to a Cistercian convent in Helfta to escape persecution. The Beguines lived communally, helping the poor and needy, outside of the control of the ecclesiastical authorities, making them a target for persecution by the clergy. Her work is most notable for using the language of courtly love in relation to Christ, portraying Him as the bridegroom with the soul as His bride. In using the form of dialogue, as opposed to the vivid visual descriptions used by earlier female Mystics, she creates a significant shift in emphasis, reflecting the cultural and social changes of her time, in particular the increasing importance of the role of the individual, the use of dialogue in philosophical discourses and the increased emphasis on rational thought in scholastic circles. She was deeply influenced, as were many Mystics of her time, by the Neoplatonic idea that the soul's true desire is to return to and be at one with the Divine, that which she called "the flowing light of the Godhead". The same theme, of the soul's ascent to God, is to be found in *The Seven Degrees of Love* by Beatrijs of Nazareth (c.1200-1268), who was brought up in a Beguine community from the age of seven following the death of her mother, becoming a Cistercian in 1215 with her two sisters and taking her vows a year later. A trained calligrapher and manuscript illuminator, she too wrote in the language of courtly love, describing in her work seven forms of love "which come from the apex and return to the summit". She speaks of transcending the material world, and her own nature, and the confines of time, as a means of entering the "profound abyss of the divinity" in order to achieve union with God. Her use of language and imagery is very tactile and corporeal, as she describes God drawing her heart into his, his presence passing through her body and his blood flowing into her soul.

All we really know of Hadewijch of Brabant, beyond her writings, is that she was Flemish and born in the 13th century. She may have been from Brabant, indicated through her use of language, or possibly Antwerp, and her letters suggest she may have been a Beguine, or lived in a Beguine community, but also lived a nomadic lifestyle. Where Mechtild wrote of the soul and Christ as bride and bridegroom, and Beatrijs used the concept of the ascent of love and the soul interchangeably, Hadewijch wrote of love as her spouse, her Mistress and her God, a bringer of pain and pleasure, ecstasy and despair. It is God who provides the illumination that allows you to follow his will "in accordance with the Truth of Love's laws". In her later work, she speaks of shedding the will completely, along with all worldly attachments, to attain "pure and naked Nothingness," with the purpose of becoming united with and absorbed into the Divine Essence.

Although we know a little more about the life of Julian of Norwich (c.1342-c.1423), we don't actually know her real name. The most significant English female Christian Mystic of the medieval period, she lived in turbulent times, of great division and significant social and political change, the country ravaged by the Plague in the late 1340s and early 1360s and the Peasants'

Revolt being suppressed in 1381. Like the other English Mystics of her time (Richard Rolle, Walter Hilton and the unknown author of *The Cloud of Unknowing*), she makes no mention of this chaos in her work, reflecting more on that which is beyond and outside of the impermanence of the material world. In the manner of Jutta von Spanheim, into whose care Hildegard von Bingen was placed in the early 12th century, she lived as an anchoress, enclosed in a cell adjoining the parish church of St Julian in Cornisford, Norwich, from which we get the only name we know her by. She was literally walled up for life, sealed in, with one window through which she could watch the church services and another through which she could give counsel to those who came seeking it. Living this solitary life, away from disturbance, Julian was able to dedicate her life to prayer and contemplation. In May 1373, before she became an anchoress, Julian became very unwell, to the point where she was read the last rites, and experienced a series of visions, which she called 'Showings', and which she wrote down as *Revelations of Divine Love*, the first book known to have been written by a woman in English. Following continuous "inward instruction" on its meaning, she produced a second, longer edition of the book twenty years' later. In comparing the two versions, we see a transformation of her perception, not only of her beliefs and of her understanding of God, Christ and the Trinity, but also in her understanding of herself. The main theme, among many themes, is the all-pervading nature of Divine Love and Divine Wisdom. One unusual, significant aspect of her work is that she speaks of God in an androgynous sense, as both our Father and our Mother, a theme originally touched on in the teachings of St Anselm. Although potentially heretical, the concept would not have been an unusual one, considering the influence of Neoplatonic thought on Christian Mysticism throughout the Middle Ages. Plotinus' portrayal of The One, to which we all wish to return and into which we all desire to be ultimately absorbed, is beyond anything male or female. And if God is all love, all wisdom, all powerful and all knowing, is in all things and is all things, then God is beyond personification, beyond our understanding, and beyond the parameters of the material world, yet both male and female and neither at the same time.

One of those who sought counsel from Julian was Margary Kempe (c.1373-1440), who wrote the first autobiography in the English language and lived an unusual life for a Mystic, being married with 14 children. After the birth of her fourteenth child, she sought to embrace a chaste life, but was unable to do so as women had so little control over their own lives that she needed her husband's permission to do so. Eventually, however, after three years of pleading, her husband allowed her to embrace chastity, but only on condition of her paying off his considerable debts and agreeing to eat and drink with him every Friday. She started having visions after becoming seriously ill following the birth of her first child, these taking the form of hallucinations of demons attacking her and trying to persuade her to give up her faith. She later experienced further visions of Christ, the Virgin Mary and other figures that offered her reassurance and teachings. She spent a lot of time on pilgrimages, to places such as Jerusalem and Rome, and was arrested several times in England for her eccentric behavior, which often involved crying and wailing in the streets and during church services.

Another eccentric medieval Christian Mystic was Catherine of Siena (1347-1380), who used to refer to The Devil as 'Old Pickpocket', heard demonic voices and said that, "Alas, every day I am tormented by evil spirits." She practiced severe mortification, involving fasting, scolding baths that would cover her in blisters, exposing herself to disfiguring disease, rolling in embers and binding her waist with a tight iron chain. For the last nine years of her life, she claimed to have stopped eating altogether and forced herself to survive on only half an hour's sleep a night. She started having visions at aged six, when she saw Christ wearing a papal tiara, and took a vow of perpetual virginity aged seven. When her family tried to marry her off, she refused and cut off all her hair, joined the Dominicans, became a mantellata at 16, and lived in solitude for over three years, thereafter dedicating her life to service, helping the poor and the ill. Her visions were often very distressing for her, on one occasion, for example, seeing persistent images over several days of naked men and women howling and dancing and engaging in sexual acts with each other. On another occasion, she claimed to have received a ring made from the circumcised flesh of the infant Jesus. She felt that all things came from God and that all things happened with the ultimate purpose of good, even if what was being experienced felt the opposite. For her, the ultimate Christian act was to joyfully and gratefully receive the suffering of others, in the same way as Christ suffered to receive the consequences of the sins of all mankind. Like many of the Mystics, she experienced a slow and painful death, her final months spent in despair and desolation, bedridden and in agony.

Coming right at the end of the medieval period, Teresa of Avila (1515-1582) did not perform the mortifications of many earlier Mystics, but like most felt that absolute poverty was vital to a truly spiritual and contemplative life. Fascinated by the lives of the saints, she attempted to run away from home aged seven to become a martyr, and found herself put into a convent at the age of 14 following the death of her mother. She first started seeing visions, like many Mystics, after a bout of serious illness. She had collapsed into a coma, where she'd remained for four days, after which she was unable to move for eight months, it being two years before she could do anything other than crawl about on her hands and knees. Sometime later, she had another significant experience when she saw an image of the crucified Christ and fell to her knees, sobbing and repenting and begging for His help.

One big influence on Teresa was the work of Francisco de Osuna, specifically his *Third Spiritual Alphabet*, which outlined the practice of 'mental prayer', a form of silent prayer. She was able to use this to cultivate further visions and revelations. This was an important development in Christian Mysticism, indicating a definite break from purely epiphanic visions and revelations to the use of meditational practices to actively create the conditions for visionary experiences, echoing the Neoplatonic advocation of mystical contemplation as a means to directly encounter The One. Perhaps the most important experience created through this process by Teresa was that known as the transverberation, during which she received a vision of an angel, who pierced her heart and entrails with a flaming golden spear, pushing it in and out of her. "The pain was so great, that it made me moan," she wrote, "and yet so surpassing was the sweetness of this excessive pain, that I could not wish to be rid of it." This lasted several days, during which time she "went about as if beside myself" and wished "only to cherish my pain". Every so often, in the ensuing years, she would go back into a trance state and experience this again "whenever it was our Lord's pleasure … which I could not prevent even when I was in the company of others". Despite her many mystical experiences, she was down to earth and practical, placing above such things the helping of others and the practice of humility, piety and compassion. She further founded the Discalced Carmelite Order, establishing seventeen convents and four monasteries between 1562 and 1582.

Disadvantaged from an early age by weird, often distressing experiences, frequently ill and feeling out of place in a world that didn't welcome or embrace strong-willed, independently-minded women, the female Christian Mystics of the Middle Ages would have been taught in their convents or cloisters that they were unworthy, inferior, inherently impure beings, descendants of the wicked temptress Eve, and this is reflected in their apologetic tone and the way they downplay their own significance, intelligence and importance, but there was a hope of redemption in emulating the grace, virtue and goodness of the Virgin Mary. Yet their visionary experiences allowed them to transcend their allocated role in life, giving them the opportunity to express themselves in a way that gave them credibility, authority and validation. What made them different was their ability to explore their spirituality in deeply personal terms. They could see a reflection of their own suffering in the crucified Christ, relating to his powerlessness, his passivity, his sense of despair and his bleeding. They were able to explore their desire for union with the Divine in a way that was physical, passionate, carnal and erotic. Whether knowingly or not, they were able to express in their work many of the secrets to be found in the Shiva-Shakti principle of the union of opposites, the Hermetic axiom of the above reflected in the below, and the esoteric symbolism in the Tantric practice of Maithuna. Their explorations resonate with us in a way that most of their male counterparts don't because they deal with many of the issues that continue to concern us as spiritual beings, and their experiential approach mirrors very strongly the contemporary desire for direct spiritual experience as opposed to a reliance on blind faith.

Hidden
Goddess

The Goddess in Folklore ~ Morgan Daimler

When the pagan religions of Europe slowly gave way to Christianity one might assume that the deities of Paganism gave way as well, but often this wasn't true. In many ways and guises they remained, hidden but still present in the awareness of the people. The Goddesses who had been such an integral part of the people's lives and beliefs did not simply disappear, nor where they all demonized by the new religion, instead they remained in the memories and stories of the people. Sometimes they were changed into the saints of the church, but in other cases they found their way into the folktales and folklore of the people, becoming instead of divine figures Fairy queens, human queens, supernatural beings, or witches. In many cases these hidden Goddesses do not neatly fit into a single category but rather move fluidly between several, being seen as both a Fairy Queen and a banshee, for example, or being connected to both a human figure as well as that of a fairy woman. Sometimes they moved slowly from one to another as the folklore about them changed, and perhaps the best way to demonstrate this is to look at a variety of examples.

If we look at Ireland we find some Goddesses who became Fairy Queens. The belief in the Good Neighbors, or fairies, was strong throughout recorded history in Ireland and even in the early periods when the myths were first recorded we see references to them. By nature they were ambivalent towards people and mercurial but could be propitiated to gain a friendlier attitude. Similarly the Gods of Ireland had a sometimes hostile and sometimes friendly relationship with humans, who, according to mythology, had invaded Ireland and driven the Gods into the fairy hills to live with the fairies. In the earliest stories humans had to make a deal with the Dagda, a powerful Irish God, to preserve their crops by agreeing to make offerings of milk and grain to the Gods but in later folk belief these same offerings were given to the fairies for the same reason showing that there was a fluid understanding of the separation between Gods and fairies. It was common in the Irish myths, for example, for members of the Tuatha Dé Danann to go from being understood or named as Gods to later being referred to as people of Fairy.

For example, Áine is associated with the Tuatha Dé Danann, the Irish Gods, and is often considered an early sovereignty Goddess. She is said in myth to be the daughter or wife of the God Manannán Mac Lir and she has a specific hill, Cnoc Áine (Anglicized to Knockainey) named for her as well as several other sites throughout Ireland. Her mythology is complex but she was strongly tied to the land, particularly in Limerick, and was said to be the progenitor of different family lines who could trace their ancestry back to her and thus legitimize their claims to rule the area. Over time instead of being viewed as a Goddess she became a woman of fairy, the daughter of the fairy king Éogabul, but still the hill was associated with her and echoes of her sovereignty remained. It was as a Fairy Queen that she interacted with the mortal king Ailill Aolum and Gerald Fitzgerald the earl of Desmond. In both cases those families would later claim descent from Áine through that interaction, in which the Goddess in the guise of a Fairy Queen had a child with the mortal. As a Fairy Queen Cnoc Áine was understood as her sí, the fairy hill in which she lived. So beloved was Áine that into the last century people still held torch lit processions on her hill on midsummer in her honor.

Another way that Goddesses hide in modern folklore is in the form of pseudo-historical Queens who have clear mythic overtones. The process of a divine character being re-written by later scribes and turned into a human character is called euhemerism and is based on the idea that all mythology is rooted in actual historic events. It can be seen in most written mythologies preserved at later dates by Christian sources, writers would often attribute classical sources to the Gods of other peoples such as the Norse Gods being euhemerized as citizens of Troy who migrated; in other cases they might be tied into the Bible itself or cultures related to it, such as we see in the Lebor Gabala Erenn's explanation of the Irish mythology relating back to Noah. In this way people were able to keep the deity as a being they could acknowledge and respect, but in the disguise of a famous historic figure, however, looking at the specific stories the Goddess was usually lurking just under the surface.

An example of this is Medb. Although her origins as a Goddess are murkier and more difficult to trace, her appearances in mythology do seem to show indicators of euhemerizing. Some scholars support the idea that Medb was originally a sovereignty Goddess who was only later re-written to be a pseudo-historical human queen and point to her multiple marriages to different kings, her reputation for outrunning horses, and descriptions of her to support this. These features echo similar ones seen in known sovereignty Goddesses. It was a theme in Irish mythology for a king to need to marry, wither literally or figuratively, the sovereignty Goddess of the area he ruled over in order to secure his right to rule; even the kings of the Irish Gods themselves were generally married to or associated with known or suspected sovereignty Goddesses. Although Medb had many husbands they were all kings and it seemed that it was marrying her which assured them of the kingship; she was also known to have many lovers and had a reputation as sexually voracious which is at odds with most depictions of human women in folklore. Horses were symbols of nobility and kingship and several sovereignty Goddesses including Áine and Macha were known to take the form of a horse or to be able to outrace horses in stories, so Medb, also being faster than a horse, ties her directly to this theme.

Another example is Macha Mong Ruadh, another pseudo-historical queen who exhibits clear indications of connection to a Goddess, not only through her name but also through her actions and qualities. In her story Macha is the daughter of a king who is one of three who shares the throne of Ireland, each for 7 years at a time. Her father dies and when his turn arrives next Macha, who is his only child declares that she will rule in his stead, to which the other two kings say that they will not share the crown with a woman. Macha then takes up arms, raises an army and wins the throne in battle; when her time is up she refuses to step down since she is queen through victory at arms rather than by agreement. One of the remaining kings dies and his five sons begin fighting against her in turn; in the meantime Macha marries the final king. Eventually she goes to the five sons disguised as a leper, lures them off one by one into the woods, binds them with rope, and forces them as her prisoners to build the fort of Emhain Macha. Macha is the name of a Goddess among the Tuatha De Danann and this Macha is linked in the Dindshenchas to Macha Mongruadh. In her story we see several themes connected to sovereignty goddesses elsewhere, including the Goddess granting sovereignty to the rightful king through marriage, the Goddess appearing as a crone or old woman, and the Goddess having an important location named after her because she created or shaped it, in this case by having her enemies build a fort for her. Although Macha in this story is portrayed as a human queen and is listed in the roles of Irish monarchs it seems likely that she appears here as a Goddess in disguise, hidden in the role of a human queen but still acting as a sovereignty giver.

In other cases we see Goddesses who were named or understood as Goddesses slowly shifting into a general kind of supernatural being. This seems to be especially true of the Goddesses who had darker natures or whose purviews included things like war and death; these Goddesses who would have, perhaps, been more difficult to simply categorize as Fairy Queens instead become a fairy of a different nature, specifically the Bean Sí (Anglicized as Banshee). Although the name itself simply means 'fairy woman' the mythic being is strongly associated with death and omens of death. The Banshee specifically was a type of spirit who would appear, wailing and keening, to warn of an impending death in a family; a Banshee was usually attached to a particular family line but the folklore is diverse and can vary today.

Clíodhna is originally understood as a Goddess, a member of the Tuatha Dé Danann, often associated with Manannán and his domain, it was said that her father was Manannán's druid Gebann. In her older stories she left the Otherworld, running away with a warrior or seeking to court Aengus mac Og and ended up on the coast of Cork. Here she was known to seduce and drown young men, being particularly fond of poets. Although Clíodhna was likely originally a sovereignty Goddess of Munster in modern lore she is considered both a Fairy Queen and a banshee. In particular Clíodhna is believed to be the ancestor of several human family lines, including the McCarthys, and took on the role of banshee for them by appearing to warn of an impending death by crying for the one about to die. In this way the Goddess who began as the protector and symbolic ruler of the entire area and its inhabitants has over time become hidden in the role of a more familial figure associated closely with specific families and with the fairies of Munster.

Another Goddess figure who later came to be hidden in the supernatural role of the banshee and the related washer-at-the-ford is Badb. As a member of the Tuatha Dé Danann, Badb was one of the Morrigans and was associated with the carnage of battle, death, and prophecy. She appeared in mythology as both a woman and in the form of a crow or black bird, and as a Goddess gave prophecies. It was, I might surmise, this prophecy aspect which later evolved into the related figure of the banshee, who wailed to warn of impending death, and the washer-at-the-ford who appeared washing the bloody clothes of the doomed. The image of the Goddess gave way to that of the supernatural woman, the prophetic figure which appeared to predict death and came to be an omen of death itself. Over time the name Badb itself became a word in Irish which means both crow and in the compound Badbh chaointe means banshee.

In other cases we see the Goddess hidden in the image of mythic witches. Like the Banshee, the Goddess-turned-witch is usually a Goddess who was originally of a more dangerous or primal nature that could not be easily turned into a purely positive folkloric being. Instead she comes to occupy a position that is ambivalent in folklore, of the witch who is feared, who can help or hinder, whose assistance must be earned not by giving her offerings but by proving your own worth to her if it can be earned at all. These witches were still supernaturally powerful and retained aspects of a purely mythic nature, such as shaping the land, possessing impossible dwellings, or controlling the weather, but were not explicitly understood in folklore as deities.

Most Irish Goddesses became saints, Fairy Queens (or more general fairy women), or else were understood as generally supernatural beings but not all of them took on these roles. One in particular who was known explicitly as a supernatural witch was the Cailleach, a figure who is found in both Irish and Scottish folklore. The Cailleach, whose name in Irish means hag and witch but comes from a root meaning 'veiled one' could not easily have fit into folklore in any other role. In her oldest stories she was a powerful, primal force who may have been known by several different names which have now been lost. It is thought that she was a wife of the God Lugh, himself a king of the Tuatha Dé Danann, and that she was a sovereignty Goddess for her area who conveyed the right to rule. In later periods she was understood in folklore to be a powerful supernatural witch who shaped the land by dropping stones and by using her magic to change people and animals into standing stones. Even as a witch she is strongly connected to the harvest and harvest traditions and the last sheaf of wheat in the field was named for her. In Scottish folklore the Cailleach was a fearsome figure who ruled over winter and sought to keep the cold and snow as long as possible, until she was defeated each spring. Although in this guise she was a supernatural being and not a Goddess her divine features still shine through; the turning of the year and the weather hinged on her and her story was an endless cycle which repeated each year.

To offer a few non-Irish examples as well we can look at Slavic and Germanic folklore. In Slavic folklore we find the figure of Baba Yaga, initially listed in a 1755 book of Slavic deities but often understood as an archetypal witch figure. Sometimes Baba Yaga appears as an individual figure and other times as a group of three identically named sisters, a pattern found elsewhere among Goddesses. She is a larger than life figure who lives in a hut that walks on chicken legs and travels in a flying mortar and pestle. She is ambiguous and can both help or hinder those who encounter her. In Germanic lore we see Frau Holle who Grimm argues was originally a Goddess but who appears later as a supernatural woman, a witch and a figure associated with fairies. As a Goddess Frau Holle, who was also known as Frau Holda or Hulda, was associated with spinning and with the souls of the dead, particularly dead babies and children. She was said to travel in a wagon in procession with these souls, and to possess a mill or well into which these souls would go. In later folklore as a supernatural woman she was a leader of the Wild Hunt, a group of spirits who rode the night skies, and was also associated with the huldren, a type of fairy. Frau Holle has also had a long association with witches who were said to honor her. Like Baba Yaga, in her stories she could help or harm depending on how a person treated her, blessing one industrious girl who aided her and cursing another who was lazy. These Goddesses were still viewed as powerful even hidden in modern folklore, with snowfall attributed to Frau Holle shaking out her blanket.

The Goddess hidden in folklore wears many masks and the

examples given here are few, taken mostly from one specific culture including some general European examples.What can be seen clearly throughout all of them is that the conversion from one religion to another was not enough to encourage the people to give up their Goddesses, even the ones that had associations with more difficult things like death; rather these Goddesses were submerged into folklore and supernatural figures, taking on the guises of fairies and witches. In this way they remained a part of the people's consciousness and folklore even when religious worship turned in a different direction.

Mother Goose: The Goddesses hiding in Fairy Tales and Nursery Rhymes ~ Jeri Studebaker

Mother Goose seems as far removed from the Great Goddess as Minnie Mouse from the Queen Mother of England. Who'd ever suspect that under Mother Goose's often apologetic and unbecoming exterior lies the Master of the Universe, the Mother of All That Is? Through the years, artists have depicted Mother Goose as an aging, powerless old woman, usually thin as a toothpick or plump as a pin cushion. Often her nose hangs like a hook over her pointed chin. The Great Goddess, on the other hand, is the antithesis of this. Even as She ages Her physical beauty overwhelms us, and in Her hands She holds the powers of the universe.

Although artists generally paint Mother Goose as harmless and ineffectual, Mother in some cases possesses a few fairly awesome powers. For example, in the one and only nursery rhyme we have about her, "Old Mother Goose When She Wanted to Wander", she flies through the air on a goose as easily as cowhands ride horses across the prairie. What's more, she brandishes a powerful magic wand in the poem, using it to dig her son Jack out of the scrapes he gets into.

Mother Goose possesses a magic wand in *Harlequin and Mother Goose* too, a play written in 1806 by an itinerant British country actor, Thomas Dibdin. In this play she gives her wand to Harlequin, who uses it to change a mail box into a lion's head, make a live duck fly out of a pie, turn a tree into a statue of himself, and order a table to rise from floor to ceiling. Mother possesses deity-like powers in Dibdin's play: not only can she control the weather (she raises a storm over the village in which the play takes place), she even exercises control over life and death (raising a woman from the dead in the village graveyard).

In short, Mother Goose is not the simpleton artists often make her out to be. As a matter of fact, she appears to be a cousin of the magnificent Neolithic bird goddess of Southeastern Europe, with some suggesting that her hooked nose is a vestigial bird's beak. More than one Neolithic clay figurine from this corner of the world sports a woman's body topped by the head of a bird, and dropping south then east into Egypt we find Neolithic Egyptian artists too producing bird-goddess figurines. The latter are as elegant as swans, with svelte human bodies, arms spread out like fluttering wings topped with avian heads.

But in addition to ancient bird goddesses, Mother Goose is strongly connected to more recent female deities. For example, like Mother Goose, Aphrodite too flew through the air on the backs of geese. On the side of an ancient cup from Athens, the Greek Pixtoxenos Painter showed Aphrodite sailing through the sky on the back of a white goose. Likewise, a terracotta figurine from Tarentum, Italy, from around 380 BCE and now in the British Museum, also shows Aphrodite riding on the back of a goose, or swan, this time with her son Eros.

Another Mother-Goose-like Goddess is Holda. A Germanic deity, Holda packs such a punch even today that people still tell stories about Her. Like Mother Goose, Holda is associated with children (and conception, pregnancy, birth, child rearing, etc.). And like Mother Goose in Dibdin's play, Holda too controls the weather, making the snow fly by shaking Her (goose?) feather pillows out of the window. Perchta, Her counterpart in southern Germany, possesses the webbed foot of a goose.

Interestingly enough, at some point after the fall of the Roman Empire these two Mother-Goose-like deities – Aphrodite and Holda/Perchta – merged into one and the same goddess in the minds of Medieval Europeans.

Fairy Tales: Entering the Hidden Mind of the Great Mother

In America Mother Goose is linked with nursery rhymes and in Europe with fairy tales. Both kinds of literature are sacred, revealing much heretofore unknown about the "mind" of the ancient Great Pagan Goddess of Europe. Let's not mince words, here: most of the old fairy tales are indeed Pagan, and many are specifically about Goddesses. The Brothers Grimm knew this and said as much. And renowned Jungian scholar Marie-Louise von Franz says fairy tales come from "the realm of the gods" while German culture historian Heide Gottner-Abendroth notes that fairy tales are veiled religious myths, many of which deal with the Sacred Marriage between the Goddess and her *heros* (to be discussed later). What's more, in 2013 one of the most respected of all modern students of fairy tales, Dr. Jack Zipes, Professor emeritus at the University of Minnesota, dropped a literary bombshell: in the early Middle Ages, said Dr. Zipes, Europe's goddesses were "transformed" into fairy tale characters. These goddesses had to be hidden somewhere, or they would not have survived.

So what shiny new baubles of information can we learn about the Great Goddess from Her fairy tales? The information is in code, of course. Some trick had to be devised to keep the medieval power elite from discovering who was still walking with the Goddess, or heads would have rolled. So what is the code? For starters the fairy-tale "princess" is code for "the Goddess," and "prince" is often code for "the *heros*" or mortal lover of the Goddess. Here's a short list of other fairy tale code words and their meanings:

Apple: 1. The healing arts; 2. Aphrodite's fruit of love and death
Apple tree: The horticultural arts
Bread: The agricultural arts

Cloth, clothing: Spinning; weaving arts

Dead mothers: Goddesses, in the Otherworld

Dragon: Death; in patriarchal tales it is a symbol of the Goddess herself, who is to be conquered

Egg: The world egg, from which all things emanate

Female rivals: A patriarchal add-on

Glass coffin; glass mountain: The mountain or castle in which the Goddess resides; she can be seen there but not touched, a situation that spins Her *heros* into a love trance.

Gold: Fertility in every sense; the richness of life

Golden ball: Aphrodite's golden apple of love

Men turned into animals and then back again: The death-return aspect of the Sacred Marriage of the ancient Great Goddess religion

Mirrors: Magic cultic knowledge

Oven: The agricultural arts

Poetic verses: Can be magic spells

Prince: The Goddess's *heros* (sacred marriage partner)

Princess: 1. The Goddess; 2. A priestess, or earthly representative of the Goddess

Red, black and white: The three sacred colors, symbol of the triple Goddess (sends the *heros* into a love trance)

Sister, youngest: In many parts of pre-patriarchal Europe it was the youngest sister who inherited the family wealth

Sleep, extended: Journey into the Otherworld

Snakes: 1. Death; 2. Death goddess; 3. The phallus. In tales altered by the patriarchy snakes become negative symbols of the Goddess, who is to be conquered

Spindle, spinning: Fate; destiny

Well: A gateway to the Otherworld

Witch: Death goddess. Converted into a malevolent hag by the patriarchy

In the fairy tale Snow White you'll stumble across several of the above code words and phrases: "princess", "apple" (poisoned), "dead mother", "glass coffin", "red" in combination with "white" and "black" and " mirror". Primarily the code reveals this as a story about the Sacred Marriage (Hieros Gamos), the romance between the Goddess and her *heros*. Each year, so that life on earth might continue, the Goddess mates with Her chosen human. Originally, all such tales would have included the entire annual cycle: the marriage, the *heros'* death, his resurrection, and finally his competing again to become – for another year – the apple of the Goddess's eye.

Two coded phrases in Snow White symbolize things that drive the Goddess's *heros* mad with desire: "glass coffin" and the color combination red, black and white. While she's protected in her glass coffin, the *heros* can see Snow's ruby-red cheeks, her ebony-black hair, her pearly-white complexion, but he cannot touch her. And this simply drives him up a wall.

In Sleeping Beauty are the following code words and phrases: "prince", "princess", "fairy godmother", "spinning", "flax" and "100-year sleep". The Sleeping-Beauty story is about the Goddess fated to trek through the Otherworld (her 100-year "sleep") before being awakened, kissed, and made love to by her *heros*. She then gives birth to twins, Sun and Moon – a fact omitted, of course, from the Disney version of the tale.

Other fairy tales too are about the Sacred Marriage – The Frog Prince, for example, The Goose Girl at the Well, and The Glass Mountain. But not all are. Like goddesses, magic too was forbidden by law during the Middle Ages and had to be disguised in some way to survive. I believe many fairy tales – especially those containing rhyming verses – are actually coded magic spells. Our European ancestors considered rhymes almost as potent as bullets or bombs. The Celts, for example, believed words could raise welts on your face and even kill you.

One example of a tale that might have been a magic spell is Rumpelstiltskin. If so, it would have been a spell for child protection in which the magic practitioner chanted the words of the tale's famous rhyme:

Today I bake, tomorrow brew,
The next I'll have the young Queen's child.
Ha! glad am I that no one knew
That Rumpelstiltskin I am styled!

In place of "the young Queen", the practitioner would substitute the name of the mother of the child to be protected, and in place of "Rumpelstiltskin" his or her own name.

Jack and the Beanstalk could be a coded spell for winning wealth or good luck. Remember its rhyme, shouted out by the wealthy giant?

Fee-fi-fo-fum,
I smell the blood of an Englishman!
Be he alive, or be he dead,
I'll have his bones to grind my bread!

At the end of the tale you'll remember that Jack inherits the giant's wealth. And like Jack, the recipient of the magic spell too would be expected to gain wealth.

Almost every fairy tale includes objects that could be useful incantation paraphernalia. Jack has beans, of course, but also bones and bread (see the rhyme above). In the Rumpelstiltskin tale are bread, beer, pig bones, sheep bones, a necklace and a finger ring.

Other fairy tales with rhymes include Kate Crackernuts – a healing spell? Donkeyskin – a spell against sexual predators? Molly Whuppie, perhaps a spell for retrieving lost possessions. The True Bride – maybe a spell for winning back a lost lover; the Swan Maiden tales, spells for conceiving children; The Juniper Tree, maybe a spell for healing a sick child.

A Kinder, Gentler World

But what makes fairy tales and nursery rhymes as fragrant as flowers in springtime is their focus on things in short supply in today's patriarchal world: social equality, warlessness, laughter, adventure, creativity, curiosity, kindness, and more. No true fairy tale is about war. And fairy tales sing with the message that we're all equally valuable, even if we aren't smart (Dummling in the Golden Goose), aren't pretty (Kate Crackernuts, the Beast in Beauty and …), or aren't young (many fairy tales include old men and women valued for their wisdom).

Likewise, the fairy tale poor are on equal footing with the rich. Many fairy tale protagonists are poorer than church mice (Jack of the Beanstalk, for example, and Hansel and Gretel), and yet are considered as worthy as the wealthy, well-manicured characters in the tales. And although many fairy tale heroines are as capable as any man, we don't hear much about them – modern publishers and media moguls shun powerful female characters in favor of passive ones like Sleeping Beauty and Snow White (who, as we've seen, actually represent the Goddess carrying out Her conjugal role in the Sacred Marriage).

Patriarchal societies seem suspicious of pleasure, and often view pain as the road to personal growth. In contrast, fairy tales put great stock in romance, physical beauty, and other sensual pleasures. More than one tale, for example, centers on the importance of laughter (The Golden Goose, The Twelve Brothers, The Six Swans, and The Twelve Wild Ducks, for starters). And strikingly gorgeous fairy tale women are legion: Cinderella, Sleeping Beauty, and Snow White, of course, but also Beauty in Beauty and the Beast, the Goose Girl, and almost all fairy tale princesses.

Another thing the Goddess tells us through Her fairy tales: all things possess spirit, and all things therefore are to be respected. In The Straw, the Coal, and the Bean, for example, three inanimate objects seem as alive as any human. And when a woman pulls straw and coal out to build a fire to cook her beans, each of these three "objects" trembles in the face of death. Each feels compassion for the other; all three think complexly, all engage in mutual cooperation, and so forth. And in the tale Mother Holle, bread baking in an oven and apples hanging on a tree are animate beings crying out in fear and for help; the Goddess (Mother Holle) rewards the character Marie for rescuing the bread from the oven and shaking the apples down from their tree.

Nursery Rhymes as Mind of Goddess

The Goddess whispers to us too through Mother Goose's nursery rhymes. Not through all of them; many are purely patriarchal. The following six, however, are without a doubt straight from the mind of the Great Mother.

> *Hey Diddle Diddle,*
> *The cat and the fiddle*
> *The cow jumped over the moon.*
> *The little dog laughed*
> *To see such a sport,*
> *And the dish ran away with the spoon.*

I can't begin to imagine this rhyme in the 17th-century *New England Primer*. The puritanical *Primer* taught babies the alphabet with words like "sinned", "slay", "bite" and "whipped":

> A *In Adam's Fall*
> *We sinned all.*

> B *Thy Life to mend,*
> *God's Book attend.*

> C *The Cat doth play,*
> *And after slay.*

D *A Dog will bite*
A Thief at Night.

E *The Eagle's Flight*
Is out of Sight.

F *The idle Fool*
Is whipt at School...

Hey Diddle Diddle is as different from this as candy from castor oil. It's all lighthearted silliness, rule breaking, and wild magic (cows can't jump over the moon! Unless they're magic cows, of course). It's about risk taking and adventure (the dish runs away with the spoon). It's about animals and people being equal – a cat plays an instrument we thought only humans smart enough to master.

Another "diddle diddle" rhyme from the Goddess:

Diddle diddle dumpling, my son John,
Went to bed with his trousers on,
One shoe off, and one shoe on,
Diddle diddle dumpling, my son John.

Here's a boy following his heart. So what if other boys climb into night clothes before crawling between the sheets? Doesn't mean John has to! John is a nonconformist – a trait that would easily have dumped an old New England Puritan into a state of near apoplexy.

Jack Sprat could eat no fat;
His wife could eat no lean;
So 'twixt them both they cleared the cloth,
And lick'd the platter clean.

In *The Primer,* Mother serves Father his porridge – and who knows when *she* gets to eat? But in the land of the Sprats, Mother and Father work together as a team, each equally valuable. There's no tension between Jack and his wife, only a clean plate – the result of both having their needs met.

> Ride a cock horse to Charing-Cross,
> To see a young woman
> Jump on a white horse,
> With rings on her fingers
> And bells on her toes,
> And she shall have music
> Wherever she goes.

Why is this from the Goddess? Because it's about our senses, our capacity to revel in our hearing, taste, feelings, sight and smell. And forget passive women: this one not only rides horses, she leaps onto their backs and races to the nearest trail, hungry for adventure.

The next rhyme is one of the most ancient, going back hundreds of years:

> One misty, moisty morning,
> When cloudy was the weather,
> I chanced to meet an old man
> Cloth-ed all in leather;
> Cloth-ed all in leather,
> With a strap beneath his chin.
> How do you do, and how do you do,
> And how do you do again?

The Goddess opens this rhyme in nature, Her personal realm, with "mist", "moisture", "clouds" and "weather". It's about positive human relationships, and it gives high marks to politeness, civility and subtle lighthearted humor.

"Handy-Spandy, Jacky Dandy" speaks for itself:
Handy-spandy, Jacky dandy,
Loves plum-cake and sugar candy.
He bought some at a grocer's shop,
And pleased away went hop, hop, hop.

In conclusion, it's time we looked at Mother Goose, her fairy tales, and her nursery rhymes with new eyes. Once we know the code that hides the treasure within, there's gold to be mined in these old oral traditions.

Beyond the Veil: The Goddess in Witchcraft ~ Mélusine Draco

Old Craft is not generally seen as gender specific but in truth, its beliefs do tend to lean towards the male aspect since the female element of deity remains veiled and a mystery. In other words, the 'God' is the public face of traditional British Old Craft while the 'Goddess' remains in the shadows, revered and shielded by her protector. Not because she is some shy and defenceless creature, but because face to face she would be too terrible to look upon! Or as the scientist who discovered the deadly Marburg filovirus observed when he saw the virus particles: "They were white cobras tangled among themselves, like the hair of Medusa. They were the face of Nature herself, the obscene goddess revealed naked ... breathtakingly beautiful."

One of the original concepts of the 'hidden goddess' can be found in Amunet, the pre-dynastic Egyptian Goddess of Air or Wind, whose name means 'She Who is Hidden', 'The Invisible One' or 'That Which is Concealed'. She was one of eight primeval deities who existed before the beginning of the world but was simply the feminine form of Amun's own name, depicted as a woman wearing the Red Crown of Lower Egypt. Before the First Dynasty she had been assimilated with Neith, whose primary cult in the Old Kingdom was established in Saïs by King Hor-Aha of the First Dynasty, in an effort to placate the residents of Lower Egypt by the ruler of the unified country.

The original imagery of Neith was as deity of the unseen and limitless sky and the Greek philosopher Proclus, who spent time traveling and being initiated into various mystery cults, wrote that the inner sanctum of the temple of Neith in Sais carried the following inscription: *"I am the things that are, that will be, and that have been. No one has ever lifted the veil by which I am concealed."* It is an inscription often attributed to Isis in later times but the true dedication belongs to Neith – the original hidden goddess.

In Greek mythology, it is possible that Persephone was also originally a 'hidden goddess' since Homer describes her as the 'formidable, venerable majestic princess of the underworld, who carries into effect the curses of men upon the souls of the dead'. Persephone held an ancient role as the dread queen of the Underworld, and it was forbidden to speak her name. This tradition came from her merging with the very old chthonic divinity Despoina (the mistress), whose real name could not be revealed to anyone except those initiated to her Mysteries. Also, Persephone as a vegetation goddess and her mother Demeter were the central figures of the Eleusinian Mysteries that predated the Olympian pantheon; the origins of which are uncertain, but they was based on very old agrarian cults of the rural communities.

Possibly the earliest possible representations are the prehistoric 'Venus' figurines that date from the Upper Palaeolithic period, found from Western Europe to Siberia. These items were carved from soft stone, bone or ivory, or formed of clay and fired. To date over 200 of the figurines have been found – all sharing the same characteristics of pendulous breasts, sagging stomachs and buttocks; the heads are small and featureless, i.e., without identity. The oldest is carved from a mammoth tusk and is over 35,000 years old, but despite the large numbers of figurines discovered, archaeologists are still at a loss to explain the function of these featureless women. According to anthropologist, Richard Leakey, the figures were assumed to represent a continent-wide female fertility-cult, although "recent and more critical scrutiny, however, shows a great deal of diversity in the form of these figures, and few scholars would now argue for the fertility-cult idea".

In more modern times, there are traceable elements of the Hidden Goddess or the 'Divine Feminine' in Freemasonry and the Marian Cult within the Roman Catholic Church.

In *Freemasonry and the Hidden Goddess* by William Boyd, the author has assembled a considerable amount of information and illustrations that suggested concealed goddess symbolism within Masonic imagery, despite the fact that it is seen as a male-dominated secret society. He draws a large amount of his symbolism from beautiful classical copper-plate etchings, most of which represent the different elements of Freemasonry in female form. In an age when nearly all women were deprived of education, it would possibly have made more sense to represent arts and sciences as old men with beards, which was the usual custom in the past, unless the feminine aspect played an important role *behind* the scenes.

The Virgin Mary attained cult status in the earliest centuries of the fledgling Christian Church, and despite a concerted effort begun by the Vatican forty years ago to de-emphasize her, the mother of Jesus remains a powerful, albeit polarizing, force within the Catholic Church; although the Church's liberal wing still claims the Marian Cult is an unnecessary anachronism. But why did the early Church feel a need to elevate Mary to a position of worship? Perhaps to help spread Christianity, 'since ancient people needed a feminine figure in their worship", suggests Sarah-Jane Boss in *Empress and Handmaid: On Nature and Gender in the Cult of the Virgin Mary*. "They were used to having goddesses. Moreover, virgin births of gods figured prominently in many ancient myths and pioneering Christians often piggybacked on paganism to speed conversion."

Surprisingly, despite the torturous methods of the Inquisition, the infamous *Malleus Malificarum* makes scant mention of any female deity as part of the witch-cult, and yet surely the worship of a *female* deity at that point in history would have been considered a greater, if not equal heresy than paying homage to any Devil? Even Margaret Murray's more sympathetic scrutiny of the witch-trials (*The Witch-Cult in Western Europe*) contains no reference to any 'goddess' connected to witchcraft, except for a passing mention of the decree of the Council of Ancyra, referring to 'certain wicked women ... [who] believe and profess that they ride at night with Diana'. The council dismissed these assertions as products of dreams and officially dismissed them as illusory but they were to resurface in an episcopal statute of Auger de Montfaucon, which says, *'Nulla mulier se nocturnis equitare cum Diana paganorum, vel cum Herodiade seu Bensozia, et in numina multitudinem profiteatur'*.

The introduction of Herodias, originally a biblical figure, in connection with a witch-deity was probably another intentional displacement of pagan identity. Herodias is a name linked to *stregheria,* an ancient form of Italian witchcraft, while Bensozia was *'Bona Socia'* – the 'Good Neighbour'. All these terms were titles of the Hidden Goddess and euphemisms for her real name, which was obviously never spoken aloud or the Church would certainly have recorded it for posterity. It is curious that the Church up to this point dismissed these nocturnal stories of riding to the Sabbat with the 'witch-goddess' as delusional, and the later accusations of the *Canon Episcopi* and the *Mallues Malificarum* were merely regurgitated 'facts' from much earlier texts.

In her Introduction to *The Witch-Cult in Western Europe,* Margaret Murray is frank enough to state that it was *her* choice to label 'this ancient religion the Dianic cult' in the absence of any identifiable generic name. Like the early churchmen, she had taken the image of a compatible pagan goddess with similar attributes and created a 'witch-goddess' from classical Graeco-Roman sources.

Shakespeare's three witches called upon Hecate in *Macbeth,* although some claim this as a later addition by Thomas Middleton because the extract contains stage-directions for two songs which have been found in Middleton's *The Witch,* Act V, scene ii: *'Black spirits and white, red spirits and grey, Mingle, mingle, mingle, you that mingle may'* – adaptations that often appear in both traditional witchcraft and contemporary Wicca. There is also evidence that part of this song was drawn from Reginald Scot's 16ᵗʰ-century *Discoverie of Witchcraft*, where Scott refers to *'white spirits and black spirits, gray spirits and red spirits'*.

In Charles Leyland's translation of *Aradia: the Gospel of the Witches*, Diana was named as the Tuscan goddess of the witches, whose daughter Aradia (or Herodias) was sent to earth to teach her followers the art of witchcraft and sorcery. Leland's account described an Italian legend of a woman who,

> ...traveled far and wide, teaching and preaching the religion of old times, the religion of Diana, the Queen of the Fairies and of the Moon, the goddess of the poor and the oppressed. And the fame of her wisdom and beauty went forth over all the land, and people worshiped her, calling her La Bella Pellegrina (the beautiful pilgrim).

The identity of any indigenous British goddesses, however, has been submerged beneath the influx of Romano-Celtic deities and it is extremely difficult to shake loose the tangled skein despite the fact that British Old Craft was a definite belief with customs and observances as highly developed as that of any other faith in the world. In *Chances of Death* (1897), Professor Karl Pearson visualised her as the Mother-Goddess worshipped chiefly by women but Murray claims that it was only on very rare occasions that deity appeared in female form to receive the homage of the followers. For the best part, the goddess remained hidden behind a veil of secrecy and mystery.

Traditionally, in old British witchcraft this elusive goddess is merely referred to as 'Lady' or 'Dame', titles that are also customarily taken by the female leader of the group or coven. This inaccessibility of the Hidden Goddess is due to her being, in her primitive form, too terrible to look upon; she is unapproachable simply because to do so, would mean certain death to the seeker.

This is the face of cosmic power that remains veiled to us for all time for our own safety; together with Chaos, she belongs to the first principles of the cosmos and from her were born heaven and the sea. Neither benevolent nor malevolent, the Hidden Goddess has little concern for the supplications and obsequiousness of the individual. It's said that humans create their gods in their own image but the Hidden Goddess is as far removed from us as the fantasy, as are Facebook images from our primitive tribal Ancestors. Originating in Northern Europe, she is the multi-faceted faceless image of the *matres*, a matriarchal divinity, usually represented as a trinity (now over-simplified in the maiden, mother and crone of contemporary paganism).

This Hidden Goddess might be seen as the embodiment of Gaia or Mother Nature but as Meriem Clay-Egerton described her actions:

The planet is shaking itself free, initially to try and eradicate the parasites which are disturbing it ... it is no longer a bright and proud future, but dark and sullen. The Earth realizes that to free herself she must destroy herself and start again with new building bricks. But she can't tell the guilty from the innocent, all will go as they must into infinity; the great pool of chaos.

In the future, if there is any future to come – if this environmental niche has not been blown apart or torn to pieces by the so-called dominant animal species – what would an archaeologist find to say about us? Would he consider *homo sapiens* to be a worthy holder of the planet? Or would he consider them a noisome evil spreading blight, a parasite upon the planet's surface? In all charity he would see them as a dead end: unable to progress further – totally unable to comprehend what had happened to his world – only fit to be superseded by a newer, more intelligent species ...

It may seem strange in these days of caring, sharing niceness where everyone wants to get on the witchcraft gravy train, that Old Craft witches pay homage to such a remote, uncaring and disinterested deity. How can we revere this faceless, formless, forbidding divinity that would scarcely raise an eyebrow if some cataclysmic happening wiped out humankind and replaced it with a race of highly developed rats or cockroaches?

It's quite simple as Bob Clay-Egerton explained when he described the Power of the One in pure animistic terms; that the One is everything, physical and non-physical, literally everything and therefore incomprehensible to our finite understanding. Being everything, the One is male *and* female *and* androgyne – not simply a male entity. All things are created in the image of the One because the One is every part of everything. Again, he repeats his wife's view that the One has no specific regard or concern for one species, i.e., mankind, among millions of species on one insignificant minor planet, in an outer arm of a spiral galaxy which is one among millions.

We often find that newcomers to Coven of the Scales have difficulty in dealing with such an abstract way of inter-acting with this Oneness that is both at the same time god/goddess, positive/negative, passive/active, light/dark, night/day. We may use terms such as 'the Old Lass' and 'the Old Lad' to identify the type of 'witch-power' we are summoning but it is not a photo-shop embodiment of those fantasy 'goddesses' of popular paganism.

And yet ... the Hidden Goddess of Old Craft is a tangible power that can be tapped into and channelled for magical, mystical and spiritual reasons. It is the elusive power that is released into us at the moment of Initiation when we come face to face with deity and we look on the face of the Hidden Goddess for the first and last time.

Reawakened
Goddess

The Rehabilitation of Goddess Archetypes in Contemporary Society ~ Irisanya Moon

Archetypes are not intellectually invented. They are always there and they produce certain processes in the unconscious one could best compare with myths. That's the origins of mythology. Mythology is dramatization of a series of images that formulate the life of the archetypes – Carl Jung.

Throughout time, labels and categories have used to define who we are in the world. From being a mother to a healer to a victim to a warrior, these descriptions have led to societal themes that have not always been in the best interest of those they have described. We can see this in the way that stories have been told about the gods and we can see how those stories have filtered down into difficult 'truths'. But as those labels have been challenged, a rehabilitation process has begun to emerge.

When goddess spirituality began to emerge in the 1970s in the neo-pagan movement, there was a call to change the way that the goddess, and indeed women, have been defined. Through the reclamation of stories, through the uncovering of bias in mythic texts, there was an awakening to the idea that archetypes could be reclaimed and people could become empowered once more.

One of the most striking examples of this movement is the telling of the story of Persephone. A goddess who would eventually become Queen of the Underworld, she was often portrayed as the victim, the one who was stolen from her mother and raped by Hades as part of her descent. But if we turn the page back to the time of the matriarchy, to the time when women were the ones who held the primary power in their societies, the story is different.

Instead, we see the story of Persephone as a figure who wasn't a victim; she was fully aware of what she needed to do. Hearing the cries of the souls of the dead, Persephone heeded the call and went to the underworld to take her place as Queen. She was not without choice; she was in control and while she may not have realized just what her choice would mean, she stepped forward and into her power.

But instead, we are often told the story of the seduction and rape. We are told that a male figure was the perpetrator; however, this story only came into being when society moved into patriarchal control. When men were in control, they shifted the story to suit the idea that women were weak and easily contained.

Once we are able to name the storyteller as having an impact on the way that stories are told, it becomes clear that there is healing to be done. The storyteller has their own motivation and they are swayed by what is happening in the world around them at the time. They may not realize it and they may never feel they are being moved in a certain direction.

While there are many archetypes to consider, some of the most common include: Maiden, Mother, Crone, Whore/Prostitute, Warrior, Queen, Healer, Witch, Victim, Child, and Dark Goddess. In each of these labels, society has often spoken to the negative aspects or the ways in which goddesses might be deemed dangerous—unfit for the current societal rules. Some are the ones to be feared and others are the ones to be praised. And even those judgments have flipped and switched over time.

We can look to the Whore/Prostitute as one of the archetypes with the most charge and energy of dissent. There are those that look down on the whore as the one who uses sex in order to sway others or who gives up their own sexual nature to someone else. But when we can look at the archetype as a message of power, things shift. If we are to see the sacred prostitute as one who understands the power of her sexuality, we can begin to see this as a goddess unto herself and fully residing in her authentic nature. She is the one who understands the impact of sensual acts, the one who steps in to heal those who might have had traumatic events surrounding their sexual being.

Rehabilitation does not come easily, to be sure. To take back these archetypes is to admit that things went horribly wrong in the past. To take back these archetypes is to not only challenge the past, but also what we have thought to be simply, well, true. From the way that goddesses have been portrayed in images to the way that societal forces have deified the opposite of their true nature. We are often surrounded and immersed in conflicting tales between what we read and what we feel.

Of course, in that sense the something is 'off', we begin to seek out ways to heal. Through the critical scholars and the feminist critique, we can begin to remember that stories aren't just about the goddesses—these stories are OUR stories too. While we might not go to Mount Olympus or travel to the River Styx, we do know what it's like to go to the place where powerful beings have meetings. And we know what it's like to grieve someone who has died.

Healing is a bumpy road. It is a process of self-reflection, of noticing where things are incorrect, and of going against the current grain. While this might be seen as a battle rather than a journey, there are bright spots that remind us that we are not alone. Though paganism and Christianity are often at odds, we can remember that while Jesus may be the star, Mary was also always revered as powerful in her own right.

We can also see that while Mary Magdalene was dismissed as the whore; she was also the one who was beloved in other interpretations of texts. She was also the first to witness his resurrection. The desire to correct those male interpretations of myth and story has always been present, even if it has been quieted or hidden. Her story is still hotly debated in academia and modern media, and it's one that continues to be questioned as often as it is dismissed.

Going back to the Greek pantheon, we are also alerted to

the way that Zeus was often blessed with powerful titles and archetypes, while the goddesses were often split up among their labels, with the probable intention of showing that no goddess could ever be as powerful as Zeus. Those who write the stories get to pick the victors, after all.

As the goddess worship movement continued, each of the goddesses began to be named as powerful beings. They are the initiators (Cerridwen), the lovers (Aphrodite), the healers (Brigid), the magicians (Isis), the sovereign (Rhiannon), the dark goddesses (Hecate), the destroyers (Kali), and so many more archetypes. As their stories were told and retold, with the goddesses as victors and changemakers, we begin to see the labels shift from minimizing to becoming the starting point for healing.

Again, we turn to the idea of the storytellers as those who impacted (and continue to impact) the way that stories are told. They are the ones who name the victors and the victims, and those who read the stories attach themselves to what feels true for them. This is not to say that the stories that seem to be slanted in one direction should not be considered in this conversation— far from it. Instead a reminder to be open to multiple points of view is the request and the necessity for rehabilitation.

For example, we can read in Robert Graves' several instances in which goddesses were portrayed as difficult or vengeful. But if we think about when these stories emerged, they emerged only after the area was occupied by invaders. One can surmise that perhaps this place in time required or insisted that the stories be told differently—often to the detriment of goddess worshippers. In the story of Athena and Poseidon's animosity, the people of the time were called to vote upon who would be worshiped, but while Athena won the vote, the wrath of Poseidon caused so much harm that women lost their vote, their children could no longer have their mothers' name, and the people as a whole were no longer called Athenians.

On the other hand, Carl Jung's work on archetypes seems to consider the wider history of time, with an understanding of the matriarchy's role and its influence. Though he doesn't state that the pre-Hellenic mythology is matriarchal and the classical mythology is patriarchal, many of his words seem to point in this direction. Those who have studied Jung since are also quick to point out that some of the Jungians will only go back as far as the classical mythology (a.k.a. revisionist) and thus only have one part of the story.

The archetype of 'witch' is another category in which fear seems to have played a role in its interpretation. While witches were seen as healers and wise women, patriarchy came in and took back the power of women, the witch then became seen as someone who was dangerous and evil.

Reclaiming the title of 'witch' has taken time and is still a healing in progress. Though there are many that proudly call themselves witches, the history of witch burnings shows that it wasn't all that long ago that the archetype incited fear and terror. Today, the word 'witch' is often used as a negative label for someone who is seen to be too powerful and thus someone who could take power from someone/something else.

This conversation naturally includes the idea of 'collective unconscious contents' as Jung described. There are things that we have taken into our unconscious mind that continue to impact us today. While we might not think these things in our logical brain, we are still influenced by the way that we've been taught to think. We might always, for example, look at Persephone as the child who was taken away, rather than the powerful Queen. Even with the pre-Hellenic story uncovered, there might be lingering feelings that Persephone was not claiming power ... she was given it.

The trick with archetypes in the modern day is that they often ask us to choose between good and bad qualities. We are told we cannot choose to praise the whore, since many in society see that as a role that rejects morality rather than a position of confidence in one's sexual nature. As a whole, archetypes in society seem to avoid the complexity of being. Perhaps this is because the gods are supposed to be perfect in their actions, or perhaps society feels it's more convenient to have a 'yes' or 'no' answer than one that is mired in gray. It's an argument to consider strongly as we begin to heal archetypes.

What is clear is that society is beginning to challenge the archetypes, even without bringing the goddess into the conversation. With the multiple waves of feminism and gender politics, we have begun to ask more questions and to call out inconsistencies or limitations in stories. With the exposure to more information and opinions than ever before, we have an opportunity to dive deeper into the possibility that what was once considered bad, can now be a call to power.

The refusal of labels might seem to be a personal battle for our role in society, but the Goddess is certainly involved. Whether we gather together in a ritual circle or we protest on the streets, we can actively engage in changing stories and perception.

- Research – To begin our quest for healing, it becomes crucial to be well-informed. This includes finding original texts (as much as possible) and knowing the context of each story. What was happening in those lands when the goddess stories were written down? What is happening in our world today that might be impacting the story? By talking with scholars and wise women, we can begin to see where our own interpretation of stories might need a shift or adjustment.

- Stay open – Though it might not seem like a concrete step towards rehabilitation, the more we can stay open to something else, the more we will be able to create a landscape of possibility. The more we can continue to take in new information and opinions, the more we can see where ideas have gotten stuck and where there are opportunities to expand our consciousness.

- Challenge – The more we can reach out to contradict what is being shown as 'truth', the more we can start a dialogue to boost change. The more we can speak up when things aren't being said completely or accurately, the more others will do the same. We need to be a part of how the stories are being told—especially when they are not placed into historical context. We need to point out who the authors were and how the critics might be limited in their assessments.

- Show up again and again – Rehabilitation takes time. It takes effort, and it takes being willing to show up again and again. We might hear things we don't like and we might be educated by others regarding our misinterpretations. But when we show up over and over, we claim the fact that this is not a single attempt mission. Instead, it is a way of being, questioning, and reclaiming that which ultimately limits us.

- Call upon the goddesses – By turning to goddesses for support and guidance, we bring them into this world and into this life. They want their stories to be told and they want to be remembered in all of their complexity. While they might be goddesses, the stories clearly illustrate that they had their failings and they made poor decisions. We can call to them to see which stories are true and helpful in this world today.

The great question emerges – what is the right archetype to praise? In the end, we want to know what we know and (most of us) want to be sure of what we know. Though we can research and ask questions, there does come a point where we will not find out all the answers. Much of history has been lost to time, and many sources continue to propagate things that just aren't true. But when we can't verify the information we have before us, we might need simply to be content with the idea of more questions.

Confronting story and archetypes is noble work. It is the work of mystics and the housewife, the priestess and the professional. By remembering that we are not limited by labels, we can break free of what we have been called or what we have wanted to be called. We can enable future generations to know their power.

Gaia & Nature ~ Elen Sentier

The 20th and 21st century were, and are, times of great change. For me, things got going with this massive phase-change at the end of the 19th century with Helena Blavatsky, Helena Roerich, Annie Bessant and Alice Bailey – all women, and all holding a torch for the goddess in their own ways. Between the four of them, they took great leaping strides from out of the conventions that had cordoned off perceived wisdom about magic and the goddess for 2,000 years, even if we now think of them as rather staid. Blavatsky was a Russian aristocrat, if only a minor one, who ran away from home after marrying Count Blavatsky, stuffed all her jewels in her pockets, saddled up her horse and took off a thousand miles to the Caspian Sea, took passage on a ship and ended up in New York, founding the Theosophical Society. Exciting eh? And not perhaps what you'd thought.

Helena Roerich married a fabulous artist and spent years travelling in Tibet and Manchuria while he did his hundreds of wonderful paintings. Her husband, Nicholas, designed the set for Diaghilev's Rite of Spring amongst many other wonderful projects. They came to London, met Blavatsky, joined the Theosophical Society, and then founded their own school of mysticism, Agni Yoga.

Alice Bailey began as a Christian missionary but had a terrible time with her first husband and eventually succeeded in running away from him, with her two daughters. She then got a job in a fish-canning factory to support them, and read Blavatsky's Secret Doctrine propped up in front of the ironing board each night. She too met Blavatsky, joined the Theosophical Society, and went on to found the Lucis Trust which is a very deep school of magic and psychology.

Annie Besant left her clergyman-husband, met Helena Blavatsky, joined the Theosophical Society, became a prominent lecturer for them, and eventually their president. Annie was a social reformer as well as an esotericist – you may know of her from the Bryant & May Match Girls' Strike of 1888 – and my family knew her. My great-aunt, Ursula Mellor Bright, was a social reformer too, and she, through her husband Jacob Bright, who was MP for Manchester, got the Married Women's Property Act through and so began getting us women our rights back. She, too, was a member of the Theosophical Society, along with her daughter Esther, and Esther was best friends with Annie Besant.

These women were very much trail-blazers for the reawakening of the goddess in the 20th and 21st centuries. Their advent was a real phase-change for how people saw magic in the modern world, and my family was deeply involved with them. Magic and witchery, our old British ways, have been suborned and maligned for 2000 years and it's partly through the work of those women that we now have so much more of a voice, and even that the Witchcraft Act was eventually repealed in 1951. It is things like that, physical things in the everyday world, that have enabled the goddess to "come out", to reawaken in our modern world. And for us to reawaken to her.

Alice Bailey has been particularly important for me in my current incarnation. Bailey took esotericism into psychology, and extremely well too – though I have to admit an interest as I'm a Transpersonal Psychotherapist. Bailey's work founded both the Transpersonal Psychotherapy movement, in which I trained directly with Barbara Somers and Ian Gordon Brown (the British founders), and Psychosynthesis, which was founded by one of Bailey's students, Roberto Assagioli. The transpersonal now seems to permeate through so many walks of life, not just psychology, so bringing new ways of thinking, and of seeing magic. Psychosynthesis has given deep roots to the modern Druid movement too through Philip Carr Gomm's valuable work.

I found transpersonal psychology to be a parallel path to the old British ways in which I was brought up, along with many aspects of Jung which was part of my training too. Of course, Jung began his journey in psychology doing seances with his cousin when he was a child, and always had his familiar spirit with him throughout his life. Jung's "active imagination" technique, which we also use in the transpersonal, is so like the daydreaming, our form of journeying, which I was taught from childhood by my parents and the elders of the villages where I grew up.

The word psychology comes from the Greek words for soul or spirit – Greek *psyche* means "breath, spirit, soul" – plus the word *logia* which means "study of". Psychology is a way in which the old ways can be seen and worked with in the modern world, where magic is still unacceptable and induces fear. But many psychologists still describe the soul and the spirit as constructs of the mind. The transpersonal does not. Ian Gordon Brown and Barbara Somers were very clear about this; there is always an "other" (call it what you will), the spirit which all shamanic traditions around the world know. Jung's concepts, and the transpersonal, are gradually gaining more and more followers in our modern world, because they work, they allow and enable people to connect with spirit. There is such a yearning for this amongst people nowadays; it even raises its head in politics, look at the language used by Jeremy Corbyn and the Labour Party, or Bernie Sanders in the USA. That phase-change, opened by Blavatsky, Roerich, Besant and Bailey, really has sent out its threads everywhere in the world. The goddess is awakening, coming alive to us now, and she needed this kind of help. Both psychology and science have made roads, threads, for her, although many people (on both sides) still believe there's no connection.

Threads ... that's the word I grew up with. Dad gave me the picture early one September morning when we went out into a field covered in spiders' webs all holding drops of dew. Silver and silence, that's how it was, the whole world to the me-child then was threaded with silver on which hung diamonds. *'Look,'* said Dad, *'that's how it is. The Lady sends her threads everywhere, connecting everything with everything, al round the world.'* I got it, even though at five years old I couldn't have said it like I did above, but the picture has stayed in my mind forever.

Those threads connect more than just psychology, they spin through science too. My current incarnation has offered me many opportunities to see this. I'm married to a mathematician and physicist who used to work at the Rutherford Appleton Laboratories in Oxfordshire, and who also practices radionics, and has taught healing for the NFSH for many years. That's a nice apparent dichotomy, and it brings together both science and magic. One of the first Rutherford tales Paul told me was about an experiment he was part of, counting photons moving across a vacuum. At the end of the experiment the professor in charge summed up their finds with the following words, *'It's like the ghost of a particle moving backwards in time'* ... well, there you go!

Another of my heroes of the 20th century is Dr. James Lovelock, a British Scientist and inventor who developed the Gaia theory in the late 1960's, and that's when I first read it. Again, I was stunned to find someone who saw the world as I did, as I'd been brought up to see it. Oh, not in the same language, not quite, that my parents and their friends used but perfectly understandable. It, the Gaia Theory, is a compelling way of looking at and understanding life on Earth. It argues we're far more than just "Third Rock from the Sun" racing round our star at the precarious threshold between freezing solid and burning up, at about 67,000 mph (107,000 km/h) – and that really is one helluva lick! It asserts that living organisms *and* their inorganic surroundings evolved together as a single living system, a self-regulating (homeostatic) system that organises the conditions of life on Earth. Some scientists believe the system self-regulates global temperature, atmospheric content, ocean salinity, and lots more in a sort of "automatic" fashion, similar to the autonomic nervous system. Earth is a living system, a wholeness as we perceive her in magic, the Goddess who keeps conditions on our planet just right for life. Well, at least until we humans really get going to screw it up, as we have been since the Industrial Revolution ... and actually far longer than that, since we got the whole concept of farming wrong some 10,000 years ago. Sigh!

Lovelock's Gaia Theory inspires ideas and practical applications in economic systems, policy, scientific inquiry, and lots more, and will continue to do so if we stay with what the goddess needs of us. And if we make the connections across between science, psychology and magic that all those pioneers of the 20th century spurred into action.

All during the end of the 19th and the first half of the 20th centuries came those incredible scientists who have shown us more and more of the workings of Life, the Universe and Everything. I'm talking about people like Einstein, Bohr, Rutherford, Faraday, and James Chadwick who discovered the neutron and famously said he could see no use for the particle – it's only helped understand more of the workings of the universe ... no use at all! And the lovely Dame Jocelyn Bell, a Northern Irish astrophysicist, who discovered pulsars, by accident, back in 1967. These people, and their colleagues, have all helped show us those threads my Dad showed me back in 1953, the spiders' webs with the dew-diamonds hanging from them, in a whole different way.

What does the goddess want of us now? She wants us to change our way of thinking from *either/or* to *and/and*. We must stop compartmentalising things into neat little boxes, just a tidy size not to startle us out of our comfort zones, and open the box so we can smell the coffee. We must learn to integrate not separate. We don't do shamanism at comfy weekends at nice country-house centres where it's all safe, we do it all the time, every day, while we're doing the washing up, feeding the baby, driving the car, arguing with the bank manager, and doing our everyday job. The goddess is fed up to the back teeth with being shut away in a cupboard, only taken out at weekend, holidays … when we get around to it. As everyone knows, *round tooits* are always as rare as hen's teeth so if we hang about waiting for them we never get to actually working with her. We think about it a lot, oh yes, our heads are always busy scrambling the threads like a kitten with the knitting wool, but doing it, really making it part of our everyday lives, not separating her off? Do we do that?

The goddess asks us to change our whole concept of "opposites", that's what her forerunners, harbingers, were doing for us – those women, Jung, psychology, and all those scientists. They brought the word to light, in their own ways, and offered us a whole new variety of ways of perceiving magic.

That's made me think of biology, particularly how the snowdrop pushes its way up through the frozen ground, and the snow, to be one of the first harbingers of spring. Think about that little, delicate flower now; think about how easily you can break its stem to pick it for your vase to celebrate Bridey's Day, Imbolc, the 1st of February. Now, how does something as delicate as that manage to push its way through very solid frozen soil? And how does it know that the time is right to do so? How, several inches below the surface of the soil, does it sense the sun, sense that there is enough light now each day for it to grow? We don't know the answers to these questions, not in a scientific way, not yet, but we observe it happen every year. Lovelock's Gaia theory gives us lots of clues though, which we can correlate to the old ways of magic.

Some of us also realise that snowdrop-phenomenon has been going on for several hundreds of millions of years, long before ever there were humans to observe it. That's a bit staggering! Too often we don't even try to imagine a world without humans and, when we do, we often find it too scary to contemplate. I've always been a sci-fi fan and that really helps. Sci-fi often postulates life outside of humanity so, if you read that stuff, you get used to the idea that we're not the be-all and end-all of creation. And it helps you lose the notion that humans are especially clever or even intelligent, that they can fix and control everything. For sci-fi fans, it shows us we can't even control ourselves and that every time we try to take charge of the natural world we screw it up completely.

Yes, that's another way the goddess is speaking to us now, through sci-fi. Like with Jung's *active imagination*, or the British old way of daydreaming, sci-fi helps us transport ourselves out of our everyday comfort-box and into all sorts of possibilities. Out there, in the wilds of the daydream, otherworld shows us whole new ways of being and thinking – like Lovelock's Gaia, like Schrödinger's Cat, like Heisenberg's Uncertainty Principle (but I'm not sure of that!), like Bohr's quantum engineering and Maxwell's devil who moves time. Even like my husband's "ghost of a particle moving backwards in time" ... I could go on for hours.

The goddess has made so many moves over the past couple of hundred years to help us change so that we can see, and work with, her in our everyday lives. She wants us to do this, the Earth needs us to do this. We need to take our old-fashioned concepts, long past their sell-by dates, and put them in the recycling bin. One of the things many psychologists, and pagans, know is that human beings are even worse than cats at change. My favourite poet, TS Eliot, said in his poem Burnt Norton, *"humankind cannot bear very much reality"* and by all the gods he was right. We really are bad at it ... and we must change that, the goddess needs very badly for us to change.

She needs us to get that *and/and* mentality, to integrate, to see connections rather than differences, to see how science, psychology and magic are different ways of saying similar things. Long ago I dreamed up the following adage – *what you see depends on what you're looking at and where you're looking from.* Think about that. I thank the goddess for putting it into my mind as I find it just so useful in every walk of life. Everything is just that. Try this little exercise: sit in a chair and observe the room from that place; now move to another chair and observe the room again from that place. Do this several times, so the ideas of perspective really begin to get into your bones, and you truly see how things look different depending upon where you sit. Don't, please don't, let your head come barging in with *"it's all the same really"*, it only does that because heads get so scared of not knowing! Jung had a lovely adage, *'Never know best and never know first, come from a place of unknowing'*. Ian Gordon Brown (who was my mentor for years) had one too, *'Go into everything full of expectancy but without expectations'*. And my dear old Dad had another that I love, *'Give your head sixpence and tell it to go play with the traffic!'*

All those three adages are about what the goddess wants of us, and has been trying to show us through the wonderful discoveries of the 20th and 21st centuries. It's about the meeting of opposites. Or rather the change in our minds so the things we have called opposites we now begin to see are rather two sides of one coin. That's what the goddess is about. In our old ways, here in Britain, she is never alone, she always has her guardian god with her; they are two-in-one. She is the Land and he is her Husbandman, who cares for her. We need to become like that, become her husbandman who cares for her instead of the rapist who despoils her. She is sovereign and grants him, and us, sovereignty... once we've proved we can keep up with her and truly look after her. And always, *She* is there, *She*, the goddess, is calling us through all our new modern ways. Science, technology, psychology, sci-fi, mobile phones, computers and even TV, are all hers, made from the stuff of her body. The problem is not in them but in us, in the way we use them for selfish ends instead of communicating, sharing, and growing. As Ursula le Guin says in Left Hand of Darkness, it's about "... *the augmentation of the complexity and intensity of the field of intelligent life...*" and that's what the goddess wants. It's all her stuff. She wants us to see her, but see her NOW, not as a vision from the past but here and now. And she wants us to work with her...

A Woman's Voice ~ Sherrie Almes

I think about how much we owe to the women who went before us – legions of women, some known but many more unknown. I applaud the bravery and resilience of those who helped all of us – you and me – to be here today. Ruth Bader Ginsburg, U.S. Supreme Court Justice

Women have been struggling worldwide for millennia to find and maintain their equal and firm footing in societies that have squelched girls' and women's strengths, abilities and contributions to their communities. And for millennia their journeys have been nurtured, inspired and encouraged by the persistent presence of that which guides them from within and without – Goddess, that spirit of the Feminine Divine which gives courage in the face of fear and uncertainty; inspiration in the face of doubt, and gives strength when weakened by the burdens of life, compassion in the face of cruelty, ingenuity in times of want, and creativity in times of need. Through determination she pushes to find hope in the face of despair, to build confidence when uncertain, and survives even in the most arduous of circumstances through intelligence and intuition. This knowledge, these gifts, these life experiences that every woman comes to know intimately and to see in others as well as herself are aspects of the Goddess gained and passed down through the generations.

I was always looking outside myself for strength and confidence but it comes from within. It is there all the time. Anna Freud

In the two most recent centuries, the advances have become exponential in societies around the world in mandating the inclusion of women and girls in education, religion, employment, military service, and social and political leadership roles. They have become full persons in terms of property ownership and motherhood whereas previously they were not, prevented by law as well as by custom from having equal rights to their husbands and fathers or even brothers.

Even as late as the 1970s women had to have their husbands' signature, i.e., permission, to get credit of any type. If a woman was not married, she was restricted from purchasing medical insurance that would cover pregnancy. Even the title of "Miss" or "Mrs." gave a nod to women's marital status which prompted the reintroduction of the title "Ms" in 1971 by the Women's Strike for Equality which was held to commemorate the 50th anniversary of suffrage. It has been in use ever since.

Women banded together in the United States around the middle of the nineteenth century to demand the right to vote among other things, in order to become full citizens as proffered in The Constitution. They were able finally to achieve this on August 8, 1920 when the 19th Amendment was passed which gave women the right to participate more fully in citizenship. Women in the United Kingdom were given the same voting rights as their male counterparts in 1928.

Never doubt that a small group of thoughtful, committed citizens can change the world. Indeed, it's the only thing that ever has.
Margaret Mead

In July 1848, Elizabeth Cady Stanton and four of her friends decided to do something concrete about the discontent they felt and decided to hold a two-day public convention. In their 'Declaration of Sentiments', she stated, *Now, in view of this entire disenfranchisement of one-half the people of this country, their social and religious degradation, — in view of the unjust laws above mentioned, and because women do feel themselves aggrieved, oppressed, and fraudulently deprived of their most sacred rights, we insist that they have immediate admission to all the rights and privileges which belong to them as citizens of these United States.*

These women spoke out and stood up for themselves and their sisters and daughters, for them to have the ability to have their voices heard in ways that were finally recognized by all. They demonstrated, held marches, spoke publicly, and even marched on the White House. They were, in fact, the first protest group to do so.

For their troubles, many women were beaten, arrested, ostracized, divorced by their husbands. Some, such as Alice Paul who was the founder of the National Woman's Party, were arrested and sent to the Lorton Women's Workhouse, a Federal prison in the Washington D.C. suburbs of Virginia where they were restrained and force fed after going on a hunger strike to protest their imprisonment for exercising their right of protest and free speech.

I always feel the movement is sort of a mosaic. Each of us puts in one little stone, and then you get a great mosaic at the end. Alice Paul, writer of the Equal Rights Amendment in 1923

Like the willow, she bends during the storm but does not break. With the strength of tempered steel, she persists.

Do all the good you can, by all the means you can, in all the ways you can, in all the places you can, at all the times you can, to all the people you can, as long as ever you can. Hillary Rodham Clinton

Hillary Rodham Clinton became the woman she is today largely because of her mother Dorothy's terrible childhood experiences which inspired her to fight for justice and equality. This created a drive in her to champion women and children which has been the focus of her life. She has never lost the vision that girls and women need to become full partners with boys and men if a society is to be successful and prosperous. Girls and women deserve to have all the opportunities, rights, and value that boys and men are automatically afforded.

At the U.N. Fourth World Conference on Women in Beijing in 1995, Mrs. Clinton as First Lady led the U.S. delegation where she chose to address the highly controversial topic of human rights:

> *If there is one message that echoes forth from this conference, let it be that human rights are women's rights and women's rights are human rights once and for all. Let us not forget that among those rights are the right to speak freely — and the right to be heard.*
> Hillary Rodham Clinton

My dad was ahead of his time. He treated his first child, me, a girl, like she was smart, strong, and capable. He was a feminist. He taught me how to fish. When I was three, I caught a 5-lb bass at Great Falls on the Potomac River in Virginia. It seemed to me at the time that it was almost as big as me! He taught me a full range of "boy things" such as how to use tools, including power tools; how to properly paint a house, inside and out; to properly prune bushes and trees, mow the lawn with an old-fashioned reel mower; replace roofing shingles. He taught me to drive a car safely in all types of weather; how to change the oil and do a tune-up; and made me change a tire in the driveway before letting me leave for my first solo drive at sixteen. I also learned how to tow a boat trailer, including backing down the ramp into the water.

The summer I turned eight, I helped him build a canoe in our carport (I can still smell the large chunky gravel and dirt heated by the sun, the sawdust, and paint) and then he taught me how to get in and out without capsizing as well as how to navigate with the oars when we went to the beach. He taught me "There is no such thing as a stupid question.", "If you don't ask for what you want, you definitely won't get it.", "Never start a fight, walk away if you can, and if you can't, make sure you finish it."

When I was ten, he gave me a book about Amelia Earhart, Thor Heyerdahl's 'Kon Tiki', and, at sixteen, handed me Erik von Daniken's 'Chariots of the Gods'. These three books were pivotal, life-changing, steering me in directions I most likely would not have found otherwise.

When I was moving through early puberty, he sat down with me to talk about boys, their bodies, changes and feelings, and gave me advice about how to avoid "giving the wrong impression" or being in a "compromising situation". He taught me I wasn't responsible for a boy's unwanted attention and that I didn't have to accept it. When he saw me walking through the house with my shoulders slumped he asked me why. I started to cry and told him I was attempting to hide my breasts due to teasing by the boys in my fifth-grade class who would comment on "the bumps" in my sweater and I was embarrassed. He hugged me and let me cry for a few minutes. He gently explained that I should not be embarrassed by my body, it was doing what it was meant to do: grow into a woman. He understood, he said, that since I was the first girl in my class to "develop" it was harder on me but that soon enough the other girls would catch up. Then he pushed me back, gave me a kiss on top of my head and then growled "the good posture drill": "Head up. Chin out. Shoulders back. Chest out. Belly in. Butt under. Now, go about your business!"

Later, in my thirties and forties, we had many talks about many things, including simple pleasures, regrets, joys, and pains; learning that every thing does not have the same importance as every other thing and how to best try to discern which are the ones to fight for or against.

He was not a perfect man or a perfect husband or father. No one is, are they? He was an only child of divorced parents with an abusive, even cruel, mother and a distant father, and he had six children by the time he was thirty-five. We kids were fortunate that Daddy was a "natural father", that he had strong paternal instincts. Today I see this as an aspect of the Goddess working in his life and ours. He was able to heal some of his childhood hurts by parenting his children as he would have wanted.

My father used to say that I started becoming "difficult" when I was six years old. Retrospectively, it was a compliment. I was six in 1958, a time when girls were supposed to be sweet and demure and kind of helpless, e.g., "Oh, my! I dropped my hanky..."; a time when the overall social norm was that girls would grow up, get married, become housewives and have babies. Most moms didn't have paying jobs then. My mom stayed at home until my youngest sibling (ten years younger than I) started first grade and then she worked in the school cafeteria so she could leave for work after her kids left, get home before they did, and had the same days off.

That Progressive Insurance commercial where the spokeswoman Flo is at a party set in the 1950s and is told by a man "Shhh! Men are talking." is a good example of the social mores at the time regarding how women should comport themselves. To the company's credit, unlike the mores of the time, her response is a look of disdain while she states "I'm outaa here!". The times have most definitely changed.

When the Women's Liberation Movement formed in the mid '60s, we were watching the news one night where they were talking about it, and my dad turned to me with a look of bemusement and said, "Now I know what to call you." Thank you, Daddy!

The question isn't who is going to let me; it's who is going to stop me. Ayn Rand

She was warned. She was given an explanation. Nevertheless, she persisted, These words were spoken on the floor of the U.S.

Senate in February 2017 of Senator Elizabeth Warren when she repeatedly attempted to read a letter from Mrs. Coretta Scott King, a Civil Rights activist and widow of the Reverend Dr. Martin Luther King, Jr. This is a prime example of how even today in 2017 women are being silenced when they fight for equal rights. Male senators were later permitted to read the letter without interruption.

We realize the importance of our voices only when we are silenced. Malala Yousafzai

That very thing that others' saw as weaknesses were in truth her greatest strengths: empathy, compassion, intelligence, intuition, tenderness, patience, the ability to grow, bear and nurture children with her body.

Walking through the forest the Crone meets the Mother and the Maiden, once again renewing the cycle and thus assuring the ultimate promise of a warrior goddess to preserve and protect, reaffirming her strength, resolve, resilience, and acquiring peace of mind and peace of heart in the knowledge that she honors her crone-mother by her life's work and honors her mother-maiden by having passed on her collective wisdom and grace to those who will call her ancestor.

Crone looks back over her shoulder and sees how far she's come. She sees herself in her daughter and granddaughter and knows she has served them well, has helped clear the path for them, shown them the way, given them the tools they'll need to continue clearing the way on their individual journeys all while clearing the community path for their daughters and granddaughters each in their turn.

We would never learn to be brave and patient if there were only joy in the world. Helen Keller

She turns forward again to see the clearing done by her mother and grandmothers before her. She sees the weeds of oppression and misogyny beginning to stretch their tendrils across the road toward the future and knows her work is not yet done, knows it will never be finished, knows that while she and her sisters have done much to advance the norms in their communities, modified the present, and helped to clear the way to the future generations, she must not rest long lest the roots of complacency drag against their progress. She cannot afford to be content, cannot stop striving for what she knows to be the right thing to do in securing the safety, security and autonomy of a society deserved by herself and future generations.

The peace of mind and peace of heart acquired through strength and courage, through perseverance and clear-headed determination, through compassion and empathy, through family and community have been hard-won and she knows the satisfaction of doing the right things for the right reasons. This is the Divine Feminine at her best!

Tomorrow's
Goddess

The Future is Goddess ~ Mabh Savage

Isis
Astarte
Diana
Hekate
Demeter
Kali
Inanna!

So goes the chant around so many fires at so many gatherings of witches, wiccans and pagans. Each name a chapter in the history-book of goddess worship, and each name still worshipped and revered today. Some believe that these goddesses are all one goddess. Some believe they are all aspects of the sacred feminine that is embodied within all goddess worship. Some believe they are all individual beings, each worthy of their own offerings, sacrifices and reverence. Whatever the practitioner's relationship with these goddesses, the fact is that these goddesses have survived thousands of years, some possibly since before 3000 BCE.

That's over 5000 years ago, yet a mere 2000 years ago (approximately) a Middle Eastern guy who thought we could probably be much kinder to each other and all get along a little better, started a bit of a cult, which became the spiritual basis for much of the modern, mainstream religion practiced across the globe today.

The largest religion in the world right now is Christianity, closely followed by Islam. Two Abrahamic, patriarchal religions which have been repeatedly regurgitated into ever new and adaptive forms by our modern societies; at times twisted in the name of hatred, at times used for kindness, but always in the name of *God*; of Yahweh (Jehovah) or Allah. It's inherently understood that God is male, all powerful, and alone. There are no other gods; to say so is blasphemy. There is also no companion; no counterpart: no goddess.

If you look hard enough at the Bible, there *are* the odd mentions of goddesses, such as Ashtoreth (Astarte), who Solomon followed and was denounced as evil thereafter (1 Kings 11:5 and 11:6). Artemis is mentioned as a 'man made god' who is no god at all, though in the same verse it is written that she was worshipped in Asia and across the whole world (Acts 19:26 and 19:27). In alternative translations of the Bible it is Diana that the Ephesians worshipped. From the brief mentions we see, it's clear that the goddess was the usurper; to be mocked, derided and forgotten.

To get a better understanding of why this might be, you have to look back beyond Christianity, beyond Judaism even, and spread your scope across the world. Take in the spirituality of the Palaeolithic (Stone Age) humans. Look at the oldest depiction of a human being yet discovered: The Venus of Hohle Fels. This extraordinary item is a female figure carved from a mammoth tusk, and she is possibly 40,000 years old. 40,000 years. That's approximately 20 times longer than Christianity has been around.

She has a loop which is clearly intended for a thong or similar, which tells us she is a pendant and possibly an amulet, emphasising that this figure was obviously very important and possibly sacred or protective. She was found near the world's oldest known musical instrument, a bone flute.

Scholars look at her oversized breasts and genitalia and immediately rush to the conclusion that she is all about sex; reproduction; fertility. Because that's what women are all about, right? When you can see the breasts and the vulva, they must be advertising something sexual. At least that's the current societal viewpoint, based on patriarchal morality and the lack of understanding regarding the divine feminine.

I think it's much more likely this figurine comes from a culture where it wasn't considered pornographic to bare breasts or expose vaginas. Stone Age artifacts like this one show an understanding of the sacred nature of a woman's body: the legs and arms are missing because those are not unique. All humans have arms, legs and faces. Only women have breasts and a vulva. These differences are being revered, not mocked, and this is what makes these figures sacred. Only the woman has the power to bear a child into the world, and subsequently feed it. This was once seen as a powerful magic indeed.

In today's world, under the thumb of a predominately male-led religion and society, women are told that their bodies are shameful. Menstruation is seen as disgusting, and even a weakness, despite it being a natural, biological cycle. Sex is seen as something done *to* women, rather than something they participate in. Breasts have become sexual objects, to be ogled in push up bras, and hidden away when feeding our babies. The voice of women is constantly shushed, muted, mocked and disbelieved. Yet the evidence above shows that when our species was at its most basic, women were the key to the sacred and the divine.

It is no wonder then that so many people in the modern world are turning to goddess worship as an alternative to the dry, dusty and now outdated religions that have popped up in the last several thousand years. Paganism is marked currently as one of the fastest growing religions in the world, and while not all Pagans are sole goddess worshippers, most have a great reverence for the divine feminine in some form. The most recent census figures show that over 100,000 people in the UK identify as Pagan, and approximately 1.25 million people in the USA, and that figure is growing exponentially as more people draw away from the religions they grew up with. About half of these recorded people name themselves as Wiccans, with the rest being druids, heathens and those who walk a veritable road map of other spiritual paths.

Disillusioned with destruction, people want a religion that teaches how to nurture and grow oneself spiritually. Tired of hate, people look to a source of love; not only for those around them, but for themselves. Catholics are told they are born with sin in their very essence. Goddess worshippers are told they are sacred, divine and connected to the universe. Christians are told their god forgives sin; the goddess teaches you to forgive yourself, and to make your own morals based on what is right and good; not what you are told.

It's important to understand that the goddess is not just for women. Men have it just as hard in our gender unbalanced society. Western culture in particular states that men should be strong and bread winners; women should be kind and motherly. But what happens when the man becomes a father and wants to stay at home with his child? In the UK, they can do this for two weeks, and only within the first 56 days of the baby's birth. Mothers in the UK can take off up to a year, depending on their employer. When it is built into our very government that fathers are not as important as mothers, you can understand why men as well as women are looking for alternatives. The Goddess smiles on all her children, male and female alike, and is likely baffled at the notion that a man would be considered weak for crying, being emotional or, as above, wanting to spend time with their child; time you can never get back.

Faults like these in our political system is exactly why Goddess worship is the future. So many of our policies and procedures in western politics come from men; male religion, male leaders of church and male leaders. It is the ever-present belief that man is superior, which stems from the relatively new belief that God is a man, that has spun our world into turmoil. Yet we can still hear the voice of the Goddess, even via the deeds of those who may not consider themselves worshippers.

The voice of the goddess speaks through every man who

calls another man out for harassment; through every man who protects another person from violence; through every father who sings their baby to sleep while the mother is hard at work; every man who protests against politicians who want to take away the rights of women; through every guy who takes a stand against homophobia, transphobia, racism and all other forms of prejudice. The goddess is about equality, and equality is about empowering men as well as women, regardless of sexual preference or color. Empowering them to be the best that they can be; to escape the skewed standards of societal expectation, and stand firm as protectors of the earth and its children, hand in hand with each other, and with women and children who all believe the same.

What a family that would be for the future. Children taught the sacred nature of the earth in school. Not through dogma, or doctrine, but through sinking their tiny hands into the earth and feeling it grow. Let them spend an afternoon in the forest, turning over stones, finding beetles and worms, watching life in all its many forms and understanding their connection to each little piece. Let them write about what makes them happy, be that sunbeams, rainbows, a moonlit night or quiet time alone, and share that with their friends and family. Let parents come into school, meet each other, to truly understand the impact their presence has on their young ones. Mothers and fathers and parents and partners, working together with teachers to train our kids to be kind to the world, compassionate with each other, and strong, safe and confident.

What a world it would be when a church Sunday is a drive to the beach, to feel the power of Hekate Einalian, or Oceanic Hekate, in the sea breeze tracing fingers through your hair, and the waves lapping persistently at your feet. Perhaps you would sense the presence of Lí Ban as a gull soars overhead. Instead of wine and wafers, blood and flesh, you taste sea spray and gritty bits of sand between your teeth, and you know it is your own flesh that is divine; your own spirit, as it connects wholeheartedly to the world, to the Goddess, and to the universe.

I see a world where the words 'In God we trust' come to have no meaning, as we realize it is foolish to place our faith in an uncaring God, and instead learn to literally worship the ground we walk on. Gaia will become our deity, in all her names, and we will be so aware that we live upon her, taking constantly, that we will learn to give back, and it will be Her who trusts in us.

This is the absolute truth; if we look after our world, She will continue to be our home for millennia to come. We must learn to do what is right, without relying on words from 'sacred' tomes; we must learn to trust in our own connection to the world, and learn morality, rather than having it thrust upon us.

Religious tomes such as the Bible or the Torah often purport to be God's word, and as such, a source of morality; a code to be followed. My own view is that they contain many fascinating stories, and can be a wealth of information about how people lived in certain times, and about the attitudes of differing groups towards each other. Examining the symbolism within the religious tales is fascinating, and I would never dismiss any religious volume as useless, as they can help us understand how other people relate to their own spirituality, as well as helping us examine our own.

What we should never do, in my opinion, is take *any* written word as gospel (pardon the obvious pun) but always question and question again, to ensure we are finding the right answers to our own questions, and not just relying on the answers that may have been trotted out again and again in similar circumstances.

To accept our moral values based on the words of people writing thousands of years ago, words which have been translated and re-translated numerous times, is not a leap of faith. It is madness. Morality is subjective, and words can be twisted to have so many meanings. Look at the Ten Commandments: Honor thy father and mother. Ok, seems fair enough. But what if your mother was abusive and your father covered for her? Does the commandment still apply to you? Would a Christian who got themselves as far away from that situation and cut all ties be classed as 'not worthy'; a lesser believer? Surely no compassionate God would think so. Yet one of the axioms of the Christian world view is that the Bible is the Word of God. I don't envy anyone who has to constantly balance their real-life choices against the unbending rules of this type of God.

I much prefer the idea that we create our own personal relationship with the divine, and I truly believe that this is a major reason we are seeing a change in the world-view of the sacred. It's not just that people don't want to be told what to do. In fact, it's not that at all. People are ready to stand up and *take responsibility* for their own actions. Instead of saying 'I can't do that because it's against the word of God', people are starting to say, 'I can't do that because it's not *right.*'

Of course, some Goddess religions do have their own code of morality, but you will usually find that these are more guidelines, or aspects of morality associated with the Goddess herself. For example, the global spiritual group Covenant of Hekate has the following admired virtues: Compassion, Courage, Temperance, Justice, Wisdom.

These virtues, broadly based on Plato's cardinal virtues, are not only thought to be associated with Hekate herself, but exist to allow people across the world to support each other in the kindest and most compassionate way possible. You'll note there are no actual rules or commandments here, although the website for the Covenant does give some guidelines as to what may be expected from members with regards to each virtue. For example, alongside Compassion, we see that members are expected to show sympathy and concern towards those who may find themselves in an undesirable position. This could mean anything from standing up for someone who is experiencing online bullying, to helping the homeless in your local area. The definitions are left unspecific on purpose, to allow individuals to use the virtues in their own life with as much meaning as possible.

Humanity has had chains on for too long; the chains of false morality and 'Do as I say, not as I do' ethics. Humankind has wrongly begun to believe it is superior to the Earth and everything on it. But it has only believed this *en masse* for the past couple of thousand years or so. For thousands of years before this, humans almost gained a better understanding of the universe, because they explored it through the divinity of the female, as well as the male.

In order to redress the balance, the Goddess now needs her time. Truly, in terms of the Earth, our planet has only paused to exhale; patriarchal religion is merely the briefest moment in the lifetime of our species. The Goddess was a powerful force way before Abrahamic religion came along, and as far as I can see, from history, and humanity's current disillusion with the state of our world, it is truly inevitable that a more balanced spirituality, where the Feminine is revered as *truly* sacred, will rise again.

Foolishly, society tried to drag the goddess down, gag her and bind her, yet she never died and never fell silent. Today, her voice is louder than ever, because she knows she will return; she was just taking a breath before the song:

Isis
Astarte
Diana
Hekate
Demeter
Kali
Inanna!

The Goddess in the Machine: Worship in the Digital Age ~ Arietta Bryant

Back in the nineties, when I was just discovering Witchcraft, Wicca, and Neo-Paganism, there were only a couple of ways to meet new, like-minded folk or to find relevant information about The Craft; you either had to go to a Moot (usually held in pubs) or to look for newsletters and leaflets in New Age shops. Online networking hadn't really been thought of.

Of course, that assumed that you were lucky enough to have Moots or Pagan-friendly shops in your home town. For me, it was a mixture of luck (I overheard a conversation about a local Moot) and dogged determination (making a nuisance of myself and befriending a local market trader who sold crystals and talismans on his stall). I also read everything I could get my hands on from our local high-street bookstore. Making the "Mind, Body & Spirit" section of the shop my second home. I soaked up everything I could find on Alternative Spirituality, Magick and The Goddess. The upside of this, for me, is that I met quite a few interesting people and made some lifelong friends along the way. I have also amassed a vast library of esoteric books, from Aradia to Z. Budapest!

However, just a few years on, things are surprisingly different for today's Spiritual Seeker. In 2016, people are much more likely hop online to sate a spiritual curiosity than to visit a bookstore.

Today, a simple Google search, using the phrase '*Goddess Worship*', yields over 167 million results in a little over half a second. Now of course, not all of those sites will be relevant or trustworthy, but for the beginner it's not a bad place to start.

Of course, it hasn't always been this simple. Online networking for Pagans began to blossom in the late 90s with sites like The Witches Voice (aka WitchVox) offering a free digital bulletin board and information portal via the internet. They really were forging the way for others who came later.

Long before Facebook became the mainstay of online friendships, it was internet chat rooms and message boards which provided a safe and anonymous forum for those interested in, or already practicing The Craft. Much of the Craft practice was still "in the broom closet" and the use of avatars and made up usernames kept the identities of practitioners a secret.

The Rise of the Techno-Pagans

For many Pagans, the internet became a place to network and to research. For others, the World Wide Web became the heart of their spiritual and magickal practices. One such practitioner was Cerridwen "DragonOak" Connelly, whom I had the pleasure of meeting in 2003. Cerridwen was the first person I had ever met who used the term *Techno-Pagan* to describe their practices. Although, the term had cropped up on my radar a few years earlier in the TV show *Buffy the Vampire Slayer*. In episode 8 of series 1, "I Robot, You Jane", the Scooby Gang meet teacher Jenny Calendar who is a self-proclaimed Techno-pagan:

You think the realm of the mystical is limited to ancient texts and relics? That bad old science made the magic go away? The divine exists in cyberspace same as out here. Jenny Calendar

Outside of the fantasy of TV shows, Techno-Paganism is a term which can be used to cover many aspects of the crossover between spirituality and technology. This can include practitioners using technology in place of more traditional magickal items, substituting a Book of Shadows for a digital equivalent for example, or using your computer "Trash Folder" in the same way that a more traditional Witch might burn an item in a cauldron to release or banish it.

Perhaps the best analogy we could use here can be taken from the Hermetic concept of "As Above, So Below", which can be understood by a Techno-Pagan to mean "that which we manifest within the digital world, can also be made real within the physical world". A concept which is even easier to understand now that 3D printing is becoming ever more popular, versatile, and affordable.

Techno-Pagan Full Moon Cleansing Spell

Sit by a window with your chosen digital device. With the screen black, reflect the image of the full moon on the screen (if this is not possible – due to cloud cover, no nearby windows, time constraints etc. – you could substitute a Full Moon screen saver or wallpaper).

Concentrate on the image, feel the power of the moon filling you and your device.

Open your favourite writing application.

Create a list of the things you wish to be cleansed of. This could be bad habits, toxic relationships, a run of bad luck, illness, or addiction.

Spend time on this, give of yourself, energetically, to the spell, describe that which you wish to cleanse from yourself in as much detail as you can muster.

Read the document out loud to yourself and your God or/and Goddess.

Save the document adding "with harm to none, so mote it be" to the footer or filename.

Delete the file from your system.

As you delete it, visualise the digital code of the document, disintegrating and disbursing into the ether.

Turn your screen black one last time, reflect the moon's image in it once again. Send out a thank you to your chosen Gods.

As I write this now, at the end of 2016, I am listening to digital music, I have just used my mobile phone to control my hot water and heating, and I can check the moon phases on my smartwatch. All this I can do whilst I type a manuscript on my laptop, which is wirelessly connected to the internet, allowing me to research and create at the click of a mouse button. I imagine this would look like the very deepest of magicks indeed to someone from the past and certainly you wouldn't have to go very far back in time for this to look like science fiction.

For most of us, technology has inextricably integrated itself into our daily lives and if we can maintain a balance between the natural and the technological we can harness this in a positive way.

With so much technology at our fingertips, some people may feel that we are becoming more isolated than ever before and that with every new "friend" or "like" we are in fact becoming ever more disconnected. Personally, I disagree. Whilst I am grateful of the many real-life connections I have made through face-to-face networking, I am also aware of the freedom afforded to me by modern social media and the internet. I can keep in touch with my spiritual sister and fellow author Romany Rivers who now lives over 3000 miles away in Canada. I can arrange moots, meet-ups, rituals, and retreats with ease, and never more need I be plagued by an unanswered question in the middle of the night; most answers are now only a click away.

Cyber Covens & Web Witches

The rise in the number of Pagans actively using the internet to connect with one another has led to some interesting ritual gatherings.

When my Craft Mother, Rowann Cerridwen, passed away in 2012, there were many friends and acquaintances who wanted to attend her Funeral Rite, to honor her and to say farewell, but for reasons of health or distance could not do so. In this case it was technology which allowed us to be able to webcast the entire ritual across the internet, so that all who wanted to could watch it and feel that they were still a part of this important event.

More generally, Magickal Practitioners from all over the globe can come together, using services like SKYPE or Messenger, to hold full rituals via the internet. These rituals are certainly no less powerful just because the participants are not all in the same room. Perhaps the rituals themselves could even have the opportunity to be more powerful still because of the sheer number of people who could take part, and as I have already discussed, these online open circles are a great way to feel involved in the magickal community at times when it may not be possible for physical attendance. We live in such a busy world! Online groups truly can provide a point of connection for those who perhaps would not otherwise have the opportunity to take part in Sabbat rituals, events or networking circles.

For those looking for a more regular online Pagan experience, one which offers more than just the occasional ritual, there are a growing number of Online, or Cyber Covens operating today. I joined my first Cyber Coven at the start of the new millennium and with their support and encouragement I began my formal Priestess training. Having so few Pagan friends around me at that time, I found the online branch of The Crystal Waterfall Coven to be an invaluable step on my path, before finding a group of friends closer to home with whom to set up a Circle.

Digital Deity

So, with this rapidly blossoming network of online communities, websites and covens, where does the modern Pagan find the Goddess? Can she be found in the wires and circuitry of our computers as easily as we could find her on a windswept hillside or in the dappled shade of a forest? I like Vivianne Crowley's explanation:

> To witches, deities manifest in different ways and can be worshipped and contacted through any form suitable to local conditions and personal needs. Wicca does not believe,[...] that there is only one correct version of God and that all other God forms are false: the Gods of Wicca are not jealous Gods.
> Vivianne Crowley, WICCA: The Old Religion in The New Age

Now obviously, it's not just Wiccans for whom there is no right or wrong way to experience a personal connection with The Divine. But, if we are looking to work with Goddesses who are sympathetic to our Techno Pagan leanings or online magickal workings then perhaps it does require a little more thought to choose the best Goddess to work with. I feel that a nice place to start is to look at the established Goddesses of the past and see where they could fit within a modern lifestyle. Here are some examples:

Iris

The Olympian Goddess, **Iris**, the Rainbow Messenger, is a nice starting point. She is Goddess of Communication and also represents the link between the Gods and Humanity. Her father was Thaumus, a Sea God, and her mother was Elektra, a cloud-nymph and therefore Iris represented the connection between the two. Iris's symbol is the rainbow, which, aside from its common symbolic use to represent LGBT+ Pride, could also be interpreted to represent the vast array of different people we can now connect with, via the internet, each day. Iris is a maiden Goddess, most often depicted as a golden-winged figure wearing a traditional, Greek style, loose-fitting robe. She carries a herald's staff and a water jug.

Iris. Goddess of Communications.
Let my messages be received true and clear.
May my workings this night not be misunderstood
And may my spells not bounce back or get corrupted

Arachne

If we are searching for a deity with links to the World Wide Web, then perhaps the Greek Spider Woman, known as Arachne, could be invoked. Although she is technically not a Goddess herself, she is certainly a powerful image, and does have connections to the Gods and Goddesses of ancient Greece. A proud but boastful woman, Arachne was turned into a spider, by the Goddess Athena, following a weaving contest; therefore her sacred symbol is the web. She can also represent the skills of weaving, which again could be taken literally, or more symbolically, as in the weaving of a spell. Arachne can help us to remember to keep our ego in check when online. Arachne is also a great architype to work with if you are interested in the interconnectedness of all things.

Weaver of the Web. Aid my search,
Let me not become entangled,
In this twisted list of links,
Goddess Arachne, Spider Woman, help me find
Answers to the questions in my mind

Seshat

Anyone with an interest in Egyptian mythology will be particularly interested in my final suggestion. Seshat is the ancient Egyptian goddess of writing, creative thought and mathematics who was most noted as "she who is foremost in the house of books" which links her nicely with libraries and record keeping. She is most often shown wearing a panther skin dress, and upon her head she bears her symbol, which, although much debated, is most often seen to be a star-shaped leaf or flower, topped with downward pointing cow-horns.

Today we can look to Seshat as a literal "Goddess of the Internet". I have even seen her referred to as the 'Silicon Goddess', which again links her back to computer hardware and electronic communication. As the keeper of ancient knowledge, she can be called upon to aid with information storage devices. Seshat for me is a wonderful Goddess to link past, present, and future when considering deity in this way.

Goddess Seshat,
Keeper of the knowledge
Both ancient and new
Lend me your blessings
For this work I have to do
Silicon Goddess, Queen of the Net
Help me complete the task that's been set

We can take this idea of an Internet Goddess a step further if we consider the writings of Alexander Bard. Bard is not a Pagan, but rather an adherent to another spiritual movement called *Syntheism* within which he claims that the "the internet is God". So, if the internet is God, my Pagan logic suggests it must also be Goddess. It seems a fairly simple concept to understand.

In a future where we can pay for items in a shop with the merest flick of a smartphone, where our refrigerators can order our groceries before we realize that we needed them, and where neither distance nor language need be a barrier to friendship, the Internet can truly be seen as something otherworldly and magickal. So too can we choose to see the Goddess as the Keeper of the Library of Records, the Goddess of Communication, the Goddess of the Web ... She could so easily be all these things and more ... We could worship her as Goddess Siri, Goddess Cortana, Alexa or just as easily, Goddess Google! The Goddess is not just in the machine, she is in Everything!

The Future of the Goddess ~ Susan Harper

Throughout Her rich history, the Goddess has laughed while her demise was prematurely reported. Through countless ages, through the rise and fall of civilizations, the ebb and flow of religious movements, the emergence of philosophies and economies, She has remained. We can argue whether the contemporary Goddess and Her worship bear any resemblance at all to the ways in which She has been honored over the ages, but in the end those questions are secondary. What is important is that She remains, emerging and re-emerging and wearing the guise of whatever culture she must move, always. And now, at a moment of what seems to be cataclysmic cultural change, on a global scale, we cannot help but wonder – what is Her future? What will the Goddess look like as we move further into the 21st century and beyond, into a world that seems marked by paradigm-shattering and culture-shifting conflicts, a world in which we are grappling with the seeming rise of nationalism, fascism, and terror, a world in which much of the progress toward social justice we made in the waning years of the 20th century and the nascent years of the 21st seem to be under direct attack? If, as Cynthia Eller says, a religion with an invented past doesn't give us a future, then how do we invent and co-create the future? And what does Goddess Spirituality look like, what role does it play, in this co-creation?

Following Carol P. Christ in *She Who Changes*, I come from the standpoint that humans and the Goddess co-create the world together, and as such the future of the Goddess and humanity are both inextricable and impossible to completely determine. However, at this cultural moment, and given all that has come before, I do think that there are some fundamental qualities and trends that will shape what the Goddess looks like as we move into the next age of humanity.

The Goddess Will Be Political

Arguably, the Goddess (as all figures at the center of religion and spirituality) has always been political, and certainly the Goddess as she is known in Western culture in the Common Era is a deeply political figure. To claim a Feminine Divine in a deeply patriarchal cultural context is a profoundly political act, whether it is driven by feminist politics or not. The Goddess as I have known Her has always been an explicitly political figure, and my practice informed by Feminist Spirituality and Feminist Witchcraft as they emerged in the 1970s and 1980s in the United States. Starhawk's work, particularly *Dreaming the Dark* and *Truth or Dare*, has continuously advocated for an engaged, political activist Goddess spirituality, particularly in the NeoPagan/Wiccan paradigm. Environmental politics have also been at the forefront of much Goddess religion in the US, with former Vice President Al Gore declaring NeoPaganism "the spiritual arm of the environmental movement" in *Earth in the Balance*.

However, while Feminist Spirituality spaces have remained explicitly political – though not without their problems in this realm, which will be discussed later in this essay – much of mainstream NeoPaganism and Goddess-centered religion, certainly in the United States, has lost its political edge in the decades since 1990. In my own dissertation fieldwork among NeoPagans of various stripes in the American South, I often heard practitioners describe themselves as "not into politics" or seeing politics as directly opposed to spirituality. This is an attitude common to the New Age and New Thought movements in the United States, and indeed there has been a long tradition of associating spiritual growth with withdrawal from the concerns of the mundane world, including the political realm. Somewhere along the line, the feminist history of Goddess religion (particularly in the United States) and the revolutionary nature of the magick and witchcraft at the heart of so much

Goddess spirituality as a weapon for resistance and cultural transformation was lost, or at the very least forgotten – yet another ebb and flow of the Goddess herself, perhaps.

Since November 2016, and the shocking events of the American presidential election, however, even the most apolitical of Goddess worshipers seem to have reawakened to the need for an engaged, political, explicitly revolutionary Goddess religion, with heavy emphasis on spellwork, magick, and ritual. In the immediate wake of the election and the massive cultural shock reaction which followed, articles declaring that Witches were "leading the resistance" – particularly young, queer, and trans Witches of Color – appeared in both mainstream and alternative press. A call for a worldwide binding spell on Donald J. Trump attracted widespread attention and interest even from those who would never have considered themselves Witches. Groups like Starhawk's Reclaiming tradition, which have never ceased engaging in protest, disruptive action, and political ritual theater, as well as smaller local groups, participated in large actions such as the Women's March in 2017.

The Goddess is awake, and she is pissed, to quote a priestess with whom I work in Texas. And while not all witchcraft is Goddess-centered, and not all Goddess spirituality features witchcraft, it seems certain that going forward Goddess religion, at least as practiced in the West, will more and more be a highly politicized blend (brew, if you will) of Witchcraft, magickal practices, and intersectional feminist and leftist politics.

The Goddess Will be Intersectional

Which leads to the second characteristic of Goddess spirituality as I see it moving into the 21st century. The Goddess will be, indeed must be, intersectional. Coined by Black legal scholar Kimberle Crenshaw in the late 1980s, *intersectionality* refers to a perspective in which each individual (and every social institution) is seen as the site of multiple intersecting identities, some of which afford privilege and others of which are sites of oppression. At its most simple level, intersectionality theory encourages us to consider that race, gender, sexual orientation, class, and other identities and social locations impact people differently – people who share one identity (i.e., women share gender) may in fact experience life very differently depending on race (i.e., White women and Black women in the United States share some experiences as women, but have very different experiences with racism).

Goddess religion as its been practiced in the West, and especially the Goddess spirituality informed by Second Wave feminism in the United States, has often relied upon narratives of "universal sisterhood" or reduced women's experiences to the single domain of gender. It has also implicitly positioned White (middle-class, enabled) women as the default and assumed that Women of Color and indigenous women considered themselves "women first" and thus issues of race and ethnicity were secondary or completely unimportant. This is especially ironic given the widespread and unthinking appropriation of spiritual traditions from indigenous peoples (particularly First Nation peoples in the Americas) and African, African-American, and Afro-Caribbean traditions (such as Vodou) within the Goddess spirituality movement. Unsurprisingly many Goddess spirituality and NeoPagan spaces have been overwhelmingly if not entirely White, though there has been considerable shift in this in recent years in some communities.

The Goddess as She moves into the next age will be informed by intersectional theory and perspectives. She will require those who work with and honor her to do so in a way that is not appropriative of oppressed cultures, though there can be space for cultural exchange and appreciation in consultation with members of the communities with which practices originate – through what Lasara Firefox Allen calls being "coconspirators" rather than appropriators.

The Goddess Will be Trans and Nonbinary Affirming

Over the last decade to decade and a half, the Goddess spirituality community – again, particularly in the United States – has been divided over the issues of the inclusion of trans women and nonbinary individuals in Goddess-centered (so-called "women's spaces"). The arguments for exclusion of trans women and nonbinary people from gender-segregated Goddess spirituality spaces center on the idea that trans women do not share the experience of menstruation with cisgender women, which is central to many Goddess traditions; that trans women do not experience sexism and misogyny in the same way cisgender women do; that trans women have "male socialization" and so do not experience society "as women born women"; and that nonbinary identities essentially do not exist. These arguments are grounded in gender essentialism and bigotry, and I reject them categorically – and going into the next Age of the Goddess, I believe the majority of those who practice Goddess spirituality will as well. Already the more hardline Dianic traditions of Witchcraft, where much of the rhetoric around exclusion of trans women originates in the Goddess spirituality community, appear to be experiencing a decline due to the transexclusionary status; this seems to be driven in large part by a refusal of cisgender Gen Xers and Millennials to participate in activities or events which have transexclusionary policies.

The next Age of the Goddess will not allow for spaces that are exclusionary of trans and nonbinary people, both because it will be intersectional and political, and because it will demand liberation for all. Goddess spirituality as practiced in the 20th and 21st centuries has often been rooted in the gender binary and the gender essentialism that binary entails. The next evolution of the Goddess will require breaking that binary and questioning long-held assumptions about the very "nature" of "masculine" and "feminine." It will invite us to explore the messy middle and the margins of gender rather than relying on a neat binary. And that will entail the creation of spaces – the *co-creation* of spaces – that don't just include trans and nonbinary people in the existing frameworks of Goddess spirituality and ritual, but which *actively affirm* people of all genders by creating new frameworks and retooling existing ones to celebrate, honor, and incorporate identities both on and beyond the binary.

Does this mean that Goddess religion will eschew many of its most central rituals, such as Blood Mysteries and the Red Tent? Does it mean that, of necessity, gender-segregated spaces must be abolished? I would argue, no. But the next Age of the Goddess will see a reinterpretation of what those rituals and spaces mean, and who can and should be included in them. A move beyond gender essentialism grounded in biology and bodily configuration will be key to creating, for instance rituals that celebrate menstruation but do not exclude people of genders other than "woman" who menstruate; to creating gender liberation spaces that do not rely upon and reinforce the rigid binary that does not reflect so many people's lived experiences; to crafting rites of passage that honor not just menarche and birth and croning, but gender transitions, coming out (of various closets), claiming of gender identities beyond the binary, and more.

The Goddess Will be Decolonized and Anti-Colonial

Goddess spirituality as practiced in the West has been a largely White and White-centered movement, marked (perhaps *marred* is a better term) by colonial ideology. This most clearly presents in the appropriation of Native American/First Nations practices; practices rooted in African, African-American, and Afro-Caribbean cultures; practices drawn from Latin American healing and magickal systems; and images, symbols, and objects that come out of Hinduism and Buddhism. While not every use of these practices, objects, or symbols is inherently colonial and appropriative – cultural exchange and appreciation are real processes and it is possible for White people to engage in them – by and large the way these behaviors manifest in Goddess spirituality has been rooted in colonial ideology that is remarkably lacking in historical context or political awareness of the very real effects on the modern day populations from which these traditions, rituals, and symbols derive. A full discussion of cultural appropriation within Goddess and NeoPagan spaces and practices is beyond the scope of this article, but it is important to acknowledge this legacy, and the remarkable resistance to and fragility in the face of confronting this appropriation (let alone changing it).

In her newly (re)politicized, intersectional, inclusive and affirming guise, the Goddess will require that those who honor Her enter into these difficult dialogues and begin not just to acknowledge the problematics and harms of spiritual practices rooted in cultural appropriation, but to begin to transform them. Much like a trans and nonbinary affirming Goddess spirituality will not require the outright rejection of gendered and embodied theology, a decolonized and anti-colonial Goddess spirituality will not necessarily require that practitioners give up wholesale practices rooted in colonized cultures – sage cleansing comes readily to mind. Instead, the decolonized and anti-colonial Goddess will require that practitioners acknowledge that the practice has been appropriated, and that we either find decolonized alternatives or that we consult with colonized populations on the best way to move forward. She will require that we eschew easy excuses such as "we were all Native Americans in a past life" or "we're all one race, the human race," or "but it feels *right*" and instead engage with the fundamental power dynamics and politics that underpin such attitudes. And in Her newly (re)politicized form, the Goddess will require that we engage with the struggle for justice facing the cultures whose practices have been appropriated – from the Standing Rock

Water Protectors to Black Lives Matter and beyond.

The decolonized, anti-colonial Goddess will be increasingly of shades other than White, as Her worshipers both re(discover) the Goddesses of Native North and South America, Africa, Asia, and beyond and learn how to engage with Goddesses in these traditions in a way that does not promote appropriation and colonial attitudes. Representations of the Goddess will no longer be predominantly White and European, though those representations will remain important. In engaging with decolonization and anti-colonialism, Goddess spirituality will venerate the Goddess in all Her forms, all her many shades, all her body types, all her glorious diversity.

And the decolonized, anti-colonial Goddess will increasingly be worshiped in communities that are not predominantly White, middle-class, and Western. Certainly, there have always been people of diverse races, ethnicities, and classes that have honored the Goddess and celebrated Her rites in a variety of communities and a variety of ways. However, these spaces have often been quite separate, with many more readily visible spaces entirely or predominantly White. Addressing the legacies of appropriation and colonization within more mainstream Goddess spirituality will make Goddess spirituality spaces not just more inclusive, but more explicitly affirming and celebratory, of people outside the middle- and working-class White demographic so often associated with it, particularly in the United States.

The Goddess Will be Accessible

Alongside and intertwined with decolonization and deconstructing White supremacy and transphobia within the Goddess spirituality movement, the next Age of the Goddess will require that Goddess spaces and events be accessible – that Her people work to deconstruct barriers to access. Ableism often goes unchallenged even in Goddess spirituality and NeoPagan spaces that explicitly reject transphobia, homophobia, sexism, and racism. Especially as the movement diversifies, and as practitioners' age and have changing healthcare needs, it is incumbent to address ableism and barriers to access in these spaces and communities. The next Age of the Goddess will see increased, focused attention on seemingly mundane details such as providing movement alternatives in ritual for those with movement limitations, ensuring that ritual and festival sites are wheelchair accessible and navigable, as well as navigable by those who may have other movement or limb differences or use other mobility aids; on ensuring that those with hearing differences have access to a sign interpreter or other form of access to ritual and educational activities; that those with visual differences also have appropriate accessibility aid to ritual and educational activities; and that those with chronic illness and lifelong conditions are presented with, and invited to create and co-create, alternatives to spiritual practices which are not appropriate for them. We can see some of this in the move toward scent-free rituals at public conventions and events, the establishment of disability camps at large festivals, and the provision of sign interpreters at some large public rituals. However, these are still the exception rather than the norm. In the next Age of the Goddess, accessibility will not be a pleasant surprise because it is the exception to the rule, but will be embedded within the movement in such a way that it is (as it should be) an expectation.

The accessible Goddess will challenge the ableism inherent in much Goddess and NeoPagan theology and practice as well. Representations of the Goddess as anything other than "perfectly" bodied are rare, even when there is diversity in the shape and size of body represented. Much as it is in Western culture at large, there is often a focus on disability within Goddess and NeoPagan practice as a form of imperfection or defect. The next Age of the Goddess will require that we envision the Goddess in all the forms in which Her people come – with limb differences, with hearing and visual differences, with amputations, with chronic illness. The accessible Goddess will be, as She should always be, a reflection of the people who honor Her – and in ensuring that everyone can see a Goddess that looks like him or herself, we further promote a vision of the Goddess and Goddess spirituality which is accessible and inclusive.

Challenging ableism and creating an accessible Goddess will not just entail dismantling barriers to physical access, just as deconstructing ableism will not just be out challenging biases against physical difference. The accessible Goddess will eschew language and practices that stigmatize mental illness, that promote the idea that taking medication for mental (or other illnesses) somehow makes a person less spiritual or endangers his or her spiritual gifts, and that otherwise marginalize neurodivergent individuals. In its most obvious (and I would argue, egregious) form, in the refusal of some Wiccan traditions to initiate students who take medications for depression and other mental health conditions. However, less overt forms of ableism exist within the community, such as subtle (and sometimes overt) shaming of those who choose allopathic medication over herbs or spiritual techniques for managing mental health conditions. (This distrust of allopathic medicine and a corresponding encouragement of only "natural" cures can extend to other illnesses and conditions as well, and needs to be addressed wherever it pops up.) The accessible Goddess will not only challenge ableism, stigma, and shaming language around healthcare choices, but will also provide a context in which agency over one's own health and healthcare decisions are affirmed and supported.

The Goddess Will be Ever-Evolving

As she has over the past Ages, the Goddess in the next Age will continue to evolve. As She changes, and as the world changes, and as humans and Goddess co-create that changing world, She may take on forms and faces we cannot even conceive.

But what is for certain is that She will continue to evolve, to change everything She touches, and to be changed by the world humans co-create. Whether those changes will be for the good of all humanity, for all life, for all the planet and beyond, has yet to be written. The next Age of the Goddess will certainly be one that builds on those past Ages, but which also moves above and beyond the limitations and obstacles those Ages (and this one) present us with. The next Age of the Goddess will be one concerned with planetary survival, with bending the arc of justice, with co-creating a world in which all Her people, by whatever name they know her, live a little more free and experience a little more justice than we have in the past. But we must co-create this world with the Goddess.

The closing lines of the Reclaiming Collective circle casting say, "We stand in a place between the worlds. And what is between the worlds can change the worlds." In my circle, we have added a line: "And what can change the world is Us."

May we be prepared for the task.

Contributors

Arietta Bryant has been a practicing pagan for over twenty years. She is co-founder of Moon River Wicca, a progressive Wiccan tradition, offering classes and courses both locally and internationally. She is a contributor to *Naming the Goddess, Pagan Planet* and *Every Day Magic*. Arietta lives, in Hampshire, UK.

Dorothy Abrams is the co-founder of the Web PATH Center, a pagan church and teaching facility in Lyons, New York USA. She is the author of *Identity and the Quartered Circle: Studies in Applied Wicca* and also contributed to *Paganism 101, Naming the Goddess, Witchcraft Today 60 Years On,* and *The Goddess in America*. She is the editor of *Sacred Sex and Magick* by the Web PATH Center.

Elen Sentier grew up in the old ways of Britain through her family and the elders of the villages where she lived. She is the author of a number of books including, *The Celtic Chakras, Elen of the Ways, Trees of the Goddess* and *Merlin: Once and Future Wizard*.

Irisanya Moon is a Reclaiming Witch, initiate, priestess, international teacher, and drummer, as well as an often-vegan, shapeshifter, shadow stalker, invocateur, and Sagittarius devoted to Aphrodite, Iris, Hecate, and the Norns. She has been published in *Paganism 101, Naming the Goddess, Pagan Planet,* and *Goddess in America* and makes her living in California as a writer and magick maker. www.irisanya.com.

Jeri Studebaker is the author of *Switching to Goddess: Humanity's Ticket to the Future* and *Breaking the Mother Goose Code* She has advanced degrees in anthropology, archaeology and education and She lives near Portland, Maine, USA.

Jennifer Uzzell holds an MA in world religion specialising in the religions of Vedic India and the Hellenistic Mystery Religions. She is a senior examiner with a major UK awarding body and spent over twenty years as a head of Religious Education in the 11-18 sector. She is currently a director of an alternative funeral home in County Durham and is studying towards a PhD in the Study of Religion, investigating death rituals in contemporary Druidry.

Jhenah Telyndru holds a master's degree in Celtic Studies from the University of Wales, Trinity Saint David. She is the founder of the Sisterhood of Avalon, and her published works include *Avalon Within: A Sacred Journey of Myth, Mystery,* and *Inner Wisdom and The Avalonian Oracle: Wisdom from the Holy Isle.* Jhenah welcomes your contact through her website: www.ynysafallon.com.

Laurie Martin-Gardner is a reiki master-teacher, author, artisan and a lifelong student of myth and magick. She is the author of *Gentle Melancholy* and *To Touch the Moon* and contributed to *Naming the Goddess* and *The Goddess in America.* She lives in Alabama, USA.

Mabh Savage lives in Yorkshire, England. She is involved with several pagan groups and explores her heritage as a way to get closer to her ancestors and the world around her. She is the author of *A Modern Celt* and *Celtic Witchcraft.*

Mat Auryn is a writer, blogger, professional psychic and witch. Mat has explored various modalities of healing, energy work, and schools of occult philosophy. He has trained under world-renowned witches, conjurers and psychics such as Laurie Cabot, Christopher Penczak, Devin Hunter, Storm Faerywolf, and Chas Bogan. Mat holds the title of Priest of the White Flame in the

Sacred Fires Tradition of Witchcraft. He is an initiate, honored member and student of the Temple of Witchcraft as well as an initiate in the Cabot-Kent Hermetic Temple and a graduate of the Black Rose Witchcraft training by the Mystic Dream Academy. To learn more about Mat visit www.MatAuryn.com

Mélusine Draco originally trained in the magical arts of traditional British Old Craft with Bob and Mériém Clay-Egerton. She has been a magical and spiritual instructor for over 20 years with Arcanum and the Temple of Khem. She is the author of a number of books including the popular *Traditional Witchcraft* series. She lives in Ireland near the Galtee Mountains.

Morgan Daimler is a blogger, poet, teacher of esoteric subjects, witch, and priestess of the Daoine Maithe. She lives in Connecticut, USA and is the author of a number of books including *The Morrigan, Fairycraft,* and *Odin.*

Robin Herne is an educator, poet, storyteller, artist, dog-owner and founder member of the Druid group Clan Ogma. He has written numerous articles for Pagan magazines and is the author of *Old Gods, New Druids, Bard Song* and *A Dangerous Place.* He lives in Ipswich, UK.

Scott Irvine has researched and honoured the Goddess for the past ten years and has written several articles about her in the pagan magazine *Chronicles.* He has contributed to the books *Paganism 101* and *Naming the Goddess.* Scott is a member of the Association for Portland Archaeology.

Shaun Johnson is a student and initiate of the Mysteries. He is a member of the Executive Committee and National Council of the Theosophical Society of England, is a Trustee of the Foundation for Theosophical Studies, and occasionally gives talks on esoteric subjects in venues across the East Midlands. His work has previously appeared in *Paganism 101* and *Naming the Goddess*, both published by Moon Books, and in other publications by Scarlet Imprint, the O.T.O. and the Theosophical Society.

Sherrie Almes lives in Alexandria, Virginia and is a priestess of Tradition of the Witches Circle, although primarily is a solitary practitioner. She has been a contributing writer in three previous Moon Books publications: *Paganism 101*, *Naming the Goddess*, and *The Goddess in America*.

Susan Harper, Ph.D is an educator, activist, advocate, and ritual facilitator and lives in Dallas, Texas, USA. She holds a doctorate in anthropology and teaches courses in anthropology, sociology, and women's studies, as well as facilitating rituals in the Feminist Spirituality and Feminist Witchcraft tradition. She serves as the Graduate Reader/Editor for Texas Woman's University.

We think you will also like...

Naming the Goddess

978-1-78279-476-9 (Paperback)
978-1-78279-475-2 (e-book)

Naming the Goddess is written by more than eighty adherents
and scholars of Goddess and Goddess Spirituality, and includes
contributions from Selena Fox, Kathy Jones, Caroline Wise and
Rachel Patterson. Part 1 is a series of critical essays focusing
upon contemporary Goddess issues. Part 2 is a spiritual
gazetteer featuring more than seventy Goddesses.

*There is something here for everyone, for those new to the Goddess
and for those who know Her.*
Carol P. Christ

We think you will also like...

Journey to the Dark Goddess

978-1-84694-677-6 (Paperback)
978-1-78099-223-5 (e-book)

Discover the powerful secrets of the Dark Goddess and
transform your depression,
grief and pain into healing and integration.

*Interesting insights, creative ideas and conscious rituals all designed
to help you understand the experiences you might have during a
Journey of Descent into the Dark Goddess realm, while you are held
there in Her Underworld, and as you Ascend out of the Underworld,
returning once again to the surface of your life.*
Kathy Jones

Other Moon Books Goddess Titles You May Enjoy

The Morrigan, Morgan Daimler
On shadowed wings and in raven's call, meet the ancient Irish
goddess of war, battle, prophecy, death, sovereignty, and
magic..
978-1-78279-833-0 (paperback)
978-1-78279-834-7 (e-book)

The Cailleach, Rachel Patterson
Goddess of the ancestors, wisdom that comes with age,
the weather, time, shape shifting and winter.
978-1-78535-322-2 (paperback
978-1-78535-323-9 (e-book)

Hekate, Vivienne Moss
The Goddess of Witches, Queen of Shades and Shadows,
and the ever-eternal Dark Muse.
978-1-78535-161-7 (paperback)
978-1-78535-162-4 (e-book)

Elen of the Ways, Elen Sentier
The reindeer goddess of the ancient Boreal forest is shrouded in
mystery,
follow her deer-trods to rediscover her old ways.
978-1-78099-559-5 (paperback)
978-1-78099-560-1 (e-book)

Rhiannon, Jhenah Telyndru
An exploration of Rhiannon that remembers her history,
reclaims her divinity, and renews a pathway into relationship
with this Welsh Goddess of Sovereignty.
978-1-78535-468-7 (paperback)
978-1-78535-469-4 (e-book)

Moon Books Goddess titles by Karen Tate

Walking an Ancient Path
Rebirthing Goddess on Planet Earth
978-1-84694-111-5 (Paperback)
Walking an Ancient Path is a breakthrough in goddess-oriented books. This book is truly a milestone in bridging the gap between mainstream beliefs and the reawakening of the Goddess that has always been known to those who practice Goddess religion. Take this book on your next trip to ancient sites, and practice the rituals and prayers within at home, abroad, and in your heart.
Rev Denise Dumars, MA

Goddess Calling
Inspirational Messages & Meditations of Sacred Feminine
Liberation Thealogy
978-1-78279-442-4 (Paperback)
978-1-78279-441-7 (e-book)
A magnificent work, carefully researched, inspiring language, beautifully organized. To anyone who can only read one good book about the Goddess, I would recommend this work. Karen Tate is in love with life, and with the ancient wisdom. A very generous author who is a sister soul in revolution.
Zsuzsanna Budapest

Voices of the Sacred Feminine
Conversations to Re-Shape Our World
978-1-78279-510-0 (Paperback)
978-1-78279-509-4 (e-book)
A wonderful book by a wonderful woman, sounding a sacred roar that rises from the rich compendium of voices within, all recovering and transmitting age-old knowledge of the Sacred Feminine - knowledge that has been hidden and denied us for far too long.
Anne Baring

MOON
BOOKS

PAGANISM & SHAMANISM

What is Paganism? A religion, a spirituality, an alternative belief system, nature worship? You can find support for all these definitions (and many more) in dictionaries, encyclopaedias, and text books of religion, but subscribe to any one and the truth will evade you. Above all Paganism is a creative pursuit, an encounter with reality, an exploration of meaning and an expression of the soul. Druids, Heathens, Wiccans and others, all contribute their insights and literary riches to the Pagan tradition. Moon Books invites you to begin or to deepen your own encounter, right here, right now.

If you have enjoyed this book, why not tell other readers by posting a review on your preferred book site.